1728Plaza#7. 60,224 words
3/18/16

Dead Men Don't Bleed

A Harley L. Sachs Mystery

Seventh in the Rose Plaza series

Dead Men Don't Bleed
A Rose Plaza Mystery

By
Harley L. Sachs

ISBN (paperback) 978-1-939381-18-7
ISBN (ebook) 978-1-939381-17-0

Books by Harley L. Sachs:
Novels

Queer Company
Never Trust a Talking Horse
The Gold Chromosome
Murder by Mail (Scratch—out!)!
Ben Zukav's Coffin
The Search for Jesse Bram Conspiracy!
Murder in the Keweenaw
The Lollipop Murder Sam in Love
StopRape.com
The Accidental Courier
The Mystery Club Solves a Murder
The Mystery Club and the Dead Doctor
The Mystery Club and the Hidden Witness
The Mystery Club and the Serial Widow
White Slave
Deliver me From Evil
Dead Men Don't Bleed
The Irwin Glass series: Betrayal, Retribution. Burnt Out
Collections of short fiction
Ahoy! Quarterdeck! (Irma Quarterdeck Reports)
Anna-Lena's Troll and other stories
Threads of the Covenant: The Jews of Red Jacket
Misplaced Persons
Non-Fiction
Freelance Non-Fiction Articles
The Misadventures of Cpl. Sachs
The 1957 Sachs Arctic Expedition
From Tent to Castle: Memoir of a Year-Long Honeymoon
IS
Chilly-Chilly BANG! How We Freelanced Through
Europe's Coldest Winter in a
VW with a Kid
Essays and Columns: 1992-2011
The Writing Life
Cartoons
Hunting the Mail Buoy and other hazards to navigation

Thanks to J.J. for the use of her initials and not her person.

"In Harley L. Sachs' latest police procedural, a transgender former Vice cop, Caryl Fox, tries to fit into his new job working as a Homicide Detective while investigating the ritualistic murder in a luxury retirement community of an 84 year old war hero. The troubled memories of his years in Vice still haunt Fox, especially when he's summoned to this nasty scene and shortly thereafter to a second murder where the tattooed body of a Vietnamese Prostitute is found dumped and brutally strangled. Fox believes the two murders are connected. He tries to convince his ex-partner of this — a converted female Islamist working Vice, whom he kind of has a crush on. This sets up the long dark journey of finding what binds the two victims and uncovering the truth behind their violent murders. For Fox this is a personal journey. Like the two victims in the story, he tries to get beyond the complications in his own life and move forward. *"Dead Men Don't Bleed,"* is more than a story about justice or revenge, more than a story about the painful memories of the Vietnam War, suffering PTSD Veterans, or the sex trade. It is a complex layering of how choices affect us throughout our lives and the repercussions and fallout on others. Here, Mr. Sachs is at the pinnacle of a long writing career. His story flows flawlessly in an uneasy, dark world of sex clubs, of people masquerading behind curtains of social acceptance, and those that make a choice not to. The book is lonely and painful. Yet, there is much heart to this story that spills out of the bloody crevices."— Doc Macomber, Author of the Jack Vu & Jason Colefield Mystery Series.

Dead Men Don't Bleed

Author's note:

It isn't easy being the only transgender male detective in the Portland, Oregon police force in spite of the city's reputation as friendly to gay, lesbian and transsexual people. That's the experience of Detective Caryl (previously Carol) Fox who transferred out of Vice because he could no longer stand the pedophiles, pimps, drug dealers, meth addicts, hookers and sex traffickers. His experience was not so different from his sometimes partner in arms, J.J. a young woman who converted to Islam and wore her head covering even if it was accompanied by a bulletproof vest. She continued to labor in Vice while Caryl Fox was yet to prove his Homicide abilities in a puzzling murder case. In the Hamilton/Nguen double murder case, their integrity and skills as detectives was about to be tested. This is how it began.

Chapter One

It was Monday morning, the start of a new week of
housekeeping. The first thing Maria Alvarez noticed
when she pushed her laden housekeeping cart from the
freight elevator on the twelfth floor of the Rose Plaza
and approached apartment 1238 was the flies. Flies
weren't common in Portland, a rather insect-free Oregon
city—if you didn't count the bedbugs that infested some
of the cheap motels or the cockroaches that hung around
the food carts. The Rose Plaza was squeaky clean, so
why the flies?

Apartment 1238 was the first on her rounds on the
twelfth floor. The Rose Plaza was four blocks long and
would have depressingly long hallways were it not for the
zigzag design that followed the contours of the hill above
it. 1238 was a choice location, for being at the short end
of the hall it commanded views of Portland on three
sides. Because it was on the top floor, there was no one
above it. At that end, the segment of hallway was short,
secluded, and quiet. The apartment across the hall on the
west side of the building was being remodeled. 1238 was
secluded, a good location out of the traffic if you didn't
want to be disturbed.

Though the building was built in the 1950's and
considered old, it was the practice of the Rose Plaza to
totally remodel every apartment before someone new
moved it. That way the place was always fresh. The
maintenance staff saw to it that it never looked seedy.
Nicks in the molding in the halls were promptly touched
up, and the carpets were never allowed to get thread bare
or faded before they were replaced, and the old carpeting
recycled.

Following her housekeeping routine, Maria parked her cart with its Swifter floor mop, bucket, cleaning supplies and vacuum cleaner in the hallway and knocked at the door of apartment 1238. There was no answer, but she heard the sound of the TV. Maybe Mr. Hamilton wasn't wearing his hearing aids. Maria hesitated and used her pass key to let herself in.

She didn't have to enter the apartment before realizing there was something or someone dead in there. She knew the smell of death. She had been a cleaner at OHSU hospital up on Pill Hill before she applied for the job at the Rose Plaza. She couldn't stand the stench of an autopsy and was glad to get the job at the Rose Plaza. People did die there, several a month, which was normal when the average age in the place was 86. But usually when someone at the Plaza did die, they were in assisted living, breathing their last in Hospice Care. Though death at the Plaza was normal, nobody ever simply rotted before being discovered..

Maria called out, "Meester Hamilton?" and stepped into the apartment. Later she would remember noticing bloody footprints on the pearl grey carpet. What she saw that made a permanent nightmare image was Mr. Hamilton handcuffed to his office chair, his mouth taped, his pajama shirt torn to expose his sliced open chest, and blood everywhere.

He had obviously been dead awhile for the flies to find him and they were having a feast.

Running on sheer adrenalin, Maria was able to contain herself long enough to retreat to her cart and throw up in her bucket. She recovered long enough to wipe her mouth on a paper towel, take a deep breath, and press the button on her radio. "Call 911. Meester. Hamilton has been murdered." Then, mercifully, she fainted.

The Rose Plaza was a familiar destination for the firemen. They were first responder EMTs. Their station was only four blocks away on Fifth Avenue and they often sent the hook and ladder and another fire truck.

Like the military where some had served, a fireman's job consisted of long periods of boredom followed by moments of intense stress. Portland didn't have that many fires and they even welcomed those calls to the Plaza.

Ever since the fire chief realized that if the departments were equipped to do the same work as ambulance drivers, there would be reimbursement for those emergency calls. The ambulance companies got $1000 for a pickup, plus mileage. The fire department was reimbursed only $300, but it was better than nothing.

Being so close by, the firemen were often the ones to shift the Rose Plaza casualties to a gurney and take them to the OHSU emergency room, just up Marquam hill five minutes away. In this case, they could not. Mr. Hamilton must first be seen by the detectives. The firemen were sent away, disappointed. They did not even know who Mr. Hamilton was and why anybody would want to cut him up.

Everyone living on the east side could see the flashing lights of the fire trucks parked in the driveway. That was a common occurrence, but when the police cars showed up, it was not normal and interests piqued. The gossip mongers were instantly active. The police! War it another burglary? Or worse?

The fire department didn't come for the rare burglary. Usually they came for medical emergencies. If someone died it was usually the fire department that came, the huge hook and ladder, and a second fire vehicle, plus the ambulance, all creating a traffic jam at the entrance ramp to the Rose Plaza complex. But the police?

Katherine Seller had been hanging out near the front desk when the firemen arrived. She squeezed into the cramped elevator along with three beefy guys and rode with them to the twelfth floor. Two policemen in uniforms were in the next car. When they emerged on the twelfth floor she saw they wore standard issue bulletproof vests, each with a firearm and taser. She noticed that they also had those new body cameras.'

Was she being filmed? She self-consciously adjusted her green Monday beret and tucked a strand of hair under it. Even before the detective arrived, Katherine Seller stood in the twelfth floor hallway, pretending to be invisible so she would not be shooed away.

Katherine Seller was the last surviving member of the original mystery book club who read only mysteries written by women. After all, women were the dominant force in mystery writing. The other members of the group had gradually fallen away. Mary Higgins, ex-World War two pilot, had been murdered. Roberta Nelson died in an auto accident. Sylvia Jessup's photos had preserved the record of Rose Plaza residents even though her own memory faded. She had been denigrated to the memory management unit where she died. Wilma Peters had simply not awakened one morning. The only new member was a man, Judge Kahane, an Orthodox Jew. Well, considering Kahane's background in the law and crime he was a useful addition to the Mystery Club.

When the virtual platoon of firemen and police arrived Maria Alvarez was still unconscious and in shock. At first one of the uniforms thought she might be a victim, too, but the paramedic firemen quickly realized she had simply passed out and revived her. There was no reviving Mr. Hamilton, however. This was clearly a gruesome murder and apartment 1238 a crime scene.

The firemen were sent away.

The two uniformed police waited for a detective and the forensic team to arrive and do their thing before the body could be taken away.

It was a crowded scene in the hallway that was only wide enough for two wheelchairs to pass.

Katherine Seller watched it all. She tried to get a glimpse past the, to her mind, boyish uniformed policemen who blocked the door to Hamilton's apartment. All she caught sight of was someone in a chair and lots of blood.

Katherine had to admit to a morbid obsession with murder. She felt the thrill of the chase. There had not been an actual murder at the Rose Plaza since that business of the mobster who was bumped off in the garage and left with a canary in his mouth. Her mind started whirring like a clock that has lost its escape mechanism. This was a juicy one.

Detective Caryl Fox arrived. Katherine immediately saw through the disguise. Caryl Fox had mannish features, but this was Portland, Oregon, the unofficial capital of the LBGT folks, the lesbians, gays, and transsexuals. Katherine had read a feature in the Portland Tribune about him or her, the only sex-changed detective on the Portland police force. She, now he, had worked the vice squad for several years after being discharged from a US Army Military Police unit. Someone had figured out that he was transgender. Surgeons could remove a woman's breasts, but not create an Adam's apple throat. The Army didn't know how to deal with transgender people and gave him a medical discharge, not disabled, but with VA benefits..

To Mrs. Seller, having a transgender detective was quite a change from Detective Casey, now retired, who she knew well from their earlier cases. She wondered how she would get along with this new one. What was his name? It had been in the Portland Tribune. Caryl Fox, a simple one letter unisex conversion from Carol.

Detective Fox was wearing a dark green rain jacket long enough to cover the Glock at his hip. Katherine didn't hesitate to make her approach. "You're detective Fox, aren't you?"

The detective scrutinized the old lady. What was she? Ninety? "Either that or I've swiped someone else's badge. Who are you?"

"I'm Katherine Seller. I used to work with detective Casey on his cases before he retired."

Fox had been warned. "Seller. Yes, Casey gave me a briefing when I was promoted from the sex crimes unit.

Let me guess: you already know all about the victim in there."

"Actually, I don't. I saw the name on the door. It's Mr. Hamilton. Major Hamilton. Nobody really knows much about him. He keeps, er kept to himself. He moved to the Rose Plaza just before his wife died, leaving him with a hoarder's collection of matchbook covers and postal cards. He tried to give the collections to our Timeless Treasures store but we didn't want them. I think he just threw them out.

Fox grinned. For claiming not to know much she knew plenty. "I bet you have a dossier on everybody in the building."

"Oh, no. I just read a little sketch about Major Hamilton in the Rose Times newsletter when he moved in about four years ago. He served in Vietnam."

"No dossier then?".

Katherine shook her head and tapped her forehead. "Just my little grey cells."

"You've been reading Agatha Christie."

"Yes. I'm a fan. Of her and P.D. James."

"Well, this is a real murder, Mrs. Seller, not fiction. Please stay out of this one." Wary of this busybody, Detective Fox brushed Katherine aside and ducked under the crime scene tape to view the victim. Did every old lady want to be a Miss Marple? Still, she might be useful. Sellers must have a photographic memory to hold onto details of a four year old in-house newsletter.

Fox couldn't resist a comment. "You have a remarkable memory, Mrs. Seller."

"It's the 72 percent dark chocolate I eat every day."

"I'll be sure to add that to my diet." Before stepping into Hamilton's apartment Detective Fox turned on his long term memory to record everything he saw. In case that memory failed, he asked the police photographer who was taking digital shots of every angle of the body to photograph all aspects of the apartment.

"Get those footprints, too," he said, pointing to the smudges on the carpet. Fox would never had chosen such a light carpet. It showed every mark, which in this case would be helpful for the police. The carpet was a record of the traffic. It showed a track from the door into the living room. Fox shook his head. A carpet like that would require frequent cleaning. Impractical.

There were footprints everywhere, contaminating the crime scene.

One of the uniforms tried to follow Detective Fox into the apartment but was held back with a caution. "Wait for the forensics team. I want everything here checked for fingerprints. We don't want the crime scene contaminated." If was already too late for that.

Chastised, the cop retreated.

Studying the place where someone lived could reveal a great deal about their personality. What books did they read, if any? What pictures did they put on the walls? What souvenirs did they collect? All revealed the person who lived there. In this case, there might be a clue to who might want to kill the victim.

It was a large apartment for a single person. It had a decent kitchen if you were a cook. From the looks of the brass pots and pan hanging from hooks, this Hamilton must have been a foody. Fox couldn't see the point in elaborate cooking if you were just one person and, if Mrs. Seller was correct, something of a recluse. Maybe the kitchen ware was left over from the dead wife, hard to get rid of, kept for sentimental reasons or decoration. From the tarnish of the brass it didn't look much used.

Had Hamilton been a woman or gay there might have been souvenir refrigerator magnets and lots of kitschy knickknacks in the apartment. There were none. If Mrs. Hamilton had been a hoarder of matchbooks and clutter, Major Hamilton was Spartan. Maybe it was a reaction 1against years of tolerating his wife's hobbies. Maybe it was just because of his military background.

What about souvenirs? The only decoration on the wall of the bedroom was a military citation for a Silver Star medal mounted on a khaki-colored cloth covered board so military medals could be pinned on display. The medal was awarded to Major Aaron Hamilton for bravery in Vietnam. Fox recognized a purple heart and another that later turned out to be a good conduct medal, but one was missing. What happened to the Silver Star?

Up until then Fox had avoided approaching the stinking corpse. He drew on a pair of latex gloves and approached the victim. Hamilton had been handcuffed to the arms of an office chair, swiveled away from the desk with its PC tower computer. His legs were taped, too.

Detective Fox had learned that when Jews slaughtered an animal it was with a single cut across the throat with a knife that had no nicks in the blade, so the animal could hardly feel it until it was all over and the creature bled out. Hamilton's throat was cut, what might have been almost painless. That would have been enough to kill him in seconds, but his pajama top had been torn aside to expose his chest. A deep cut had exposed the organs under the ribs of his right side and something had been cut away. If his throat had been cut first, the incision in the chest would not have bled. Dead men don't bleed. So Hamilton had presumably been conscious when his chest was cut open.

The liver was exposed, or what remained of it. With a shudder that brought bile up from his throat, Caryl Fox realized that the killer had wanted Hamilton to be conscious, able to watch the operation. Only then was the merciful final cut across the throat administered.

It looked to Fox like a ritual murder. That put another angle to the case. The coroner could find out more.

While Detective Fox waited for the body to be zipped into a body bag and taken away on a gurney, he continued to inspect the apartment.

Was it a robbery? Hamilton's wallet with credit cards and a hundred dollars in twenties was on the chest of drawers beside his bed. Besides the cash, Hamilton had a VA health card, American Express, and Visa.

Hamilton's cell phone was also there along with car keys for an Audi. With the car key was a fob and a plastic bit from the Fred Meyer grocery. Fox knew from personal experience that every Fred Meyer purchase was recorded in Cleveland, Ohio. Kroger knew what Hamilton ate and drank. The cell phone would yield old voice mails, contact numbers, a record of Hamilton's activities. Nowadays nothing was private. Investigation would make the reclusive Major Hamilton an open book. That computer would yield his surfing habits, what he bought on line, what sites he visited. Did he collect kiddy porn?

The shallow drawer to the computer desk had the usual collection of old ball point pens and junk but also a safety deposit box key. No indication of what bank, but knowing that the Major was a recluse, it would be a good bet that it was in the Umpqua branch bank downstairs at the Rose Plaza.

The top drawer of the bedside bureau had a surprise, a neat little teak box containing Viagra, a box of condoms with several missing, and a tube of personal lubricant. Hamilton might have been a recluse, but he had a sex life. So who was his partner? Or partners?

The bed was made, tucked tightly with hospital corners in correct military style. Fox was confident that a quarter tossed onto the taut blanket would bounce. The man had been neat.

Checking the clothes closet, Fox saw that Hamilton had been obsessively tidy. He still had his military uniform, complete with a ribbon bar that was a record of where he had served. Fox didn't know which ribbons stood for what, but he would find out. The VA hospital up on Pill Hill would have his medical records with his prescriptions.

Ah, prescriptions. That was Fox's next step. The medicine cabinet in the bathroom had bottles Fox wasn't familiar with. Aspirin and anti-acids were recognizable enough.

The shower caddy had anti-dandruff shampoo, an expensive razor, and aloe shaving cream, so Hamilton shaved in the shower and had sensitive skin. The khaki colored towel hanging from the bar was dry. So when was the last shower? This was Monday. He had been dead for how long? Since Friday or Saturday? Long enough for the flies to find his body. Flies could find a corpse in ten minutes.

Detective Fox got down on his knees to look under the bed. There were no dust bunnies under it. The maid did a thorough job. How often did she do the apartment? Every week? Every two weeks? He would have to find out.

There was something under there, on the far side next to the wall. Fox had to push the double bed aside to reach it.

It was a small size woman's thong underwear, the sort worn for show, for this one was in red with a little blue flower decoration where the clitoris would be. He muttered, "Looks like Major Hamilton has had some visitors."

Where had he seen a thong like that before?

Fox rummaged through his memory like fussing through a pile of laundry in search of a missing sock. Thong underwear was uncomfortable. Since his change, Fox had worn nothing but boxer shorts. Where had he seen thongs like that?

It was something he'd seen when under cover on the vice squad. He had partnered with a female Moslem detective known only as J.J. It had been a default working relationship as they were both outcastes in a macho male organization that was only perfunctorily integrated.. They had both visited some of the so-called gentlemen's clubs. Portland had two hundred nude dancing locales, as many as it had food carts, even more than marijuana shops. But which one?

Maybe Hamilton's cell phone record would save going through two hundred nude dancing joints to find the girl who went with the thong with the blue flower.

Fox bagged the thong. It would provide DNA evidence. A nude dancer would have shaved her privates, but there would be secretions. If the owner of the thong had been booked for criminal activity, there could be a match. Trouble was, the lab was swamped, and it might take months to get the DNA report.

Fox returned to the living room. The team had arrived with a body bag and a gurney to take the body to the coroner. "Save that duct tape," Fox cautioned. "There will be fingerprints."

The tape was carefully bagged, the office chair dusted for fingerprints.

Fox thought, *"There's enough evidence here for this to be an easy case. Trouble is, we have to get enough for a trial and a conviction."* Usually the police knew who did a killing, but making a case worthy of a conviction wasn't always certain. That was up to the prosecutor and then there was the jury. You couldn't be sure. Botched evidence and the bad guy could get away with murder.

Someone had closed Hamilton's eyes. Fox looked at the dead man's face. "Looks like you didn't have such a quiet life after all, Major. Mrs. Seller will be surprised."

Chapter Two

Expecting the answer from one of the uniforms, Detective Fox asked, "Who discovered the body?"

"The maid. Maria." It was that snoopy old lady, Mrs. Seller, the one who knew all and remembered everything. "She's Cuban."

Fox had to admit Mrs. Seller was living up to what Casey had told him, warned him about. "I think you know everything Mrs. Seller."

She took it as a compliment, though it was meant to be sarcastic. She feigned modesty and shook her head. "Nor everything. I know she's been here a few months and her husband is back in Cuba depending on the money she sends him. Right now she's down the hall doing her next apartment. She gets a fixed amount of time per apartment. Has to fill out a form showing what jobs she completed. Housekeeping keeps track."

"Then she'd know if there's anything unusual or misplaced in the victim's apartment."

"She might."

Fox went to find Mrs. Alvarez.

Her cart was parked outside 1232, the door propped open according to the Rose Plaza protocol.

Fox found her scrubbing out the walk-in shower. "Excuse me, Mrs. Alvarez. I understand you were the one who found the body."

She nodded.

"Do you always clean Mr. Hamilton's apartment?"

"Every two week. I start two month ago."

"Do you also clean under the beds?"

She obviously thought the question confrontational, like Fox was accusing her of missing something. She hesitated. "Yes, sir."

Detective Fox held up the evidence bag with the thong underwear. "I found this under the victim's bed. Have you seen it before?"

She shook her head.

"I'm not accusing you of not doing your job, Maria. I just want to know if this is recent?"

"No panties under Mr. Hamilton bed."

"OK." Since she came only every two weeks, that provided a wide time frame. Fox wondered if Hamilton had been one of those fetishists, one of those creeps who collect women's underwear. Maybe the Major had a storage locker in the building full of souvenirs. He would have to look into that. "You just knocked at the door and let yourself in with your pass key?"

"Yes. Then I smell death. I see Mr. Hamilton and call 911."

"You can smell death?"

"I work before at hospital." She shrugged in the direction of OHSU.

"We will have to take your fingerprints just to eliminate yours from others we may find."

She was obviously nervous. People who committed crimes got their fingerprints taken. Immigration already had her fingerprints. Being fingerprinted made you a suspect, possibly a criminal. Being fingerprinted was an invasion of privacy. She probably knew that once fingerprinted she would be part of a national database. But she could not refuse.

Fox turned to one of the uniforms. "Get your fingerprint kit out of the patrol car for Mrs. Alvadez."

"Yes...sir," one of the uniforms said with obvious hesitation.

Fox noticed the hesitation. He thought at first the kid might have said Ma'am but caught himself. He'd become hypersensitive to all criticism of his transgender status, however subtle. Fox was tempted to say, "Get over it," but there was no point in making an issue of whether or not the young policeman accepted transgender people. They had to work together. No need to stir up nastiness. There was already enough of that.

Back in Hamilton's apartment Fox retrieved Hamilton's keys from the bedside bureau.. There were four. He checked them, tested to see which fit the lock on the apartment door. Besides a car ignition key and the safety deposit key which he had found in the computer desk, there were two others.

Hamilton's desk had a folder of bills for credit card purchases, marked "paid on line" and checked off. There was a checkbook. the check register would provide other clues to Hamilton's activity, but he didn't use many checks. "Paid on line" seemed to be the Major's way to do his business.

There was also a plastic document holder containing the major's DD 214 military record showing what his last unit was, his serial number, date of birth, weight at discharge and citations, all those service ribbons identified in the DD214. He had served in Vietnam, got the Silver Star, Good Conduct Medal, American Service medal and so on.

That was all past history. What Fox needed was who was recent history and who would want to kill him?

Before going down to the Plaza's manager's office Fox instructed the second uniform to interview everyone on the floor. "Get their names, if they knew Hamilton, and if there's been any unusual activity recently."

The hallway was crowded. The apartment next door was being remodeled, the door open, the threshold covered with taped down paper to keep plaster dust from being tracked in. It had not been effective for people had tracked plaster dust all over the hallway. The remodel crew was at work. They were two Mexicans, plasterers by the look of the gypsum on their work clothes. When they saw the police and the crime scene tape they were visibly nervous and avoided eye contact. They would have closed the door, but Fox moved right in.

The two men looked like they were afraid of being arrested. Was this detective from ICE? You could be totally innocent, but if taken in for questioning you could lose your job. They were both legally in the country or the Plaza would not have contracted for them to do the work. Still, you never knew about police. This was not Mexico, but police were police. Some were just racist thugs with uniforms and badges.

Fox showed his badge and tried to appear to be friendly, not threatening. "The man across the hall, Mr. Hamilton, is dead. Have you seen anything you might tell me about?"

Like a couple of twins, both shook their heads. It wasn't clear whether they were answering the question or simply didn't understand what Fox had asked.

Fox tried another angle. "Did you work here on the weekend? Saturday? Sunday?"

"We finish Friday. Four o'clock."

Fox gave the taller one his card. "If you remember anything we should know, call me. Understand?"

The taller Mexican nodded, took the card, looked at it like it might be infected, and slipped it in the pocket of his dirty coveralls.

"Thank you. Gracias." That was about all the Spanish Fox knew. Adjoining Washington County was 40% Spanish speaking. These guys probably lived in Beaverton. The population there was basically two tiered: well paid whites at Intel and lots of Spanish speaking farm workers outside the Portland urban growth boundary. He probably should take that crash language course.

While the victim's body was taken away in a zipped bag on a gurney in the freight elevator, Fox returned to the elevators he had ridden up in from the street. He noticed here was a security camera mounted above the elevator doors and in the elevator itself. Had there been one at the freight elevator? He hadn't noticed.

Fox stopped in at the Umpqua Bank near the Plaza entrance, showed his badge and asked if Major Hamilton had a safety deposit box. He did. But the box could not be opened unless the executor was present. The IRS was always interested in what people had in their safety deposit boxes, but usually it was junk, like an old dead one dollar pocket watch of nothing but sentimental value.

Fox asked at the reception desk about the other key. The woman at the desk, Lisa, according to the name plate on the counter, directed Fox to the management office across the breezeway.

He discovered he needed Hamilton's fob to open the door to the entrance. The door buzzed and opened. He was impressed by the Plaza security. Cameras by the elevators, fobs to get in the entrance. The neighborhood was considered a high crime area. The Plaza was a big building with lots of traffic. You had to make sure whoever wandered the halls belonged there.

The woman at the desk, nameplate Grafton, didn't recognize the visitor as police until Fox showed his badge. "Detective Fox."

MS or Mrs. Grafton brightened. "You're here about the murder of Major Hamilton."

Fox was impressed. "News follows fast in this place. Do you all watch the security cameras, too?"

She ignored the suggestion that Rose Plaza people were all snoops and busybodies. "What can I help you with?"

"For starters I need to notify the Major's next of kin. I also need to know what this key is for." He showed her Hamilton's key set.

She recognized it. "It's for a storage locker. Those are down on the first floor of the Tower."

"Could you tell me which one? I need to see the contents." Like maybe Hamilton had a stash of women's thong underwear.

"You'll need permission from the next of kin, or maybe a warrant."

"I can get that if you insist. What about the Major's next of kin?"

Mrs. Grafton locked her desk drawer and went to a filing cabinet. It was locked, too. Fox wondered, what does she think I'll do, steal her pencils or the petty cash?

He sat in the visitor's chair and waited for her to return with a slender file. She showed him the single sheet of paper. Major Hamilton had designated his son, Arthur, as his next of kin. His executor was a lawyer with an address downtown in the old Multnomah building. The son, Arthur Hamilton, lived in Syracuse, New York. He could hardly be farther away and still be in the United State. The file also included instructions for a prepaid cremation and burial in Portland's National cemetery.

"Can you make me a copy of this?"

At least she agreed to that much.

"Did he have a will?"

Mrs. Grafton confirmed that. "We have a copy on file, but you'll have to get that information from his executor."

Fox jiggled the Major's keys. Besides the fob that was the electronic key to the Plaza exterior doors, there were a car key from a Audi, the room key, the key Mrs. Grafton said was from his storage locker and a smaller one that might be from a padlock. Maybe the major had a bicycle? Possible.

Fox held up the key ring. "What's this little key for?"

"That would be his mail box."

He'd have to check on that. "Hamilton has an Audi. Do you know where it's parked?"

She looked it up. "It's on P2. Space number 43."

She was a mine of information. "Tell me about this fob gadget that I used to get in the outside door."

"The computer records who enters any of the doors and the time. It's part of security. We used to have pass keys for the exterior doors, but sometimes people would lose them. The fobs are assigned to individuals, and if one is lost we can disable it so no one can use it."

"So if someone uses this fob you know."

She nodded. "And since the time is noted, we can check the CCT camera records to see who it was that came in at that time."

Fox was impressed. "That's pretty good security for a retirement home. You'd make a good detective, Mrs. Grafton.""

"It's a high crime area. We have homeless people camping in the woods and sleeping in the park across the street."

"How long do you hold the CCT tapes?"

"A week."

"I don't know yet how long Hamilton was dead. In case that was almost a week ago maybe you could save the recordings."

She wasn't so sure about that. "They're all digital. We could probably dump the whole previous week to a computer drive and archive it."

Detective Fox reasoned that the combination of the fob record and the security cameras could catch the Major every time he entered the building. The system did not track departures. You didn't need a key to get out of the Rose Plaza. Just in.

This was going to take a lot of work and many hours. If would be easier if the killer left fingerprints and a DNA sample already on file. The murder of Major Hamilton wasn't the only killing in Portland this week. He would like a quick solution.

Fox was feeling frustrated. He was new to the homicide branch. Up to now he had tagged along with a senior detective to learn the ropes. This time he was on his own and it was his first big case. If he failed, would he be shunted back to Vice?

Caryl Fox was well aware of his tenuous situation. It was tough enough to be the only transgender detective. Even in Portland, he felt like a token, someone employed to dispel suspicions that the Portland police weren't adequately integrated. There had been a time when an African American would be the token. Now it was a transgender, just as his sometimes partner in vice,

J.J. a convert to Islam, was on the payroll. They were both subject to suspicion and occasional racist innuendo.

Dealing with his own tenuous situation, he now had a gruesome corpse to deal with and nobody knew much about the man. He wasn't one of those homeless persons found dead without any ID under the Morrison bridge. Even the homeless often had buddies. At the Rose Plaza nobody seemed to know much about Major Hamilton at all, except maybe that Mrs. Seller, but all she knew was that his wife had collected matchbooks which he then threw away after she died. That wasn't going to lead to his killer.

Hamilton had been a veteran, even a war hero if the silver star medal was a real indicator, but the Vietnam war was long ago. Caryl wasn't even born when it ended, so what did he know? It was past history.

The panties might be a clue. There should be something on Hamilton's computer hard drive. What surfing did he do? If the thong underwear was from a girl who worked at one of the two hundred nude dancing joints, someone would know more. Maybe he was a regular.

There would be the credit card records and phone records. Did he get text messages, and from whom?

It would be handy if there was a murder weapon conveniently left behind with fingerprints and DNA that was already on file, but there were none. Fox was going to have to work for his salary and affirm his legitimacy as a detective, not just someone who caught hookers soliciting on 82nd street.

The corpse would provide more information. That was up to the medical examiner.

Chapter three

The interviews of the other twelfth floor residents yielded nothing. Those old people were not exactly shut-ins, but they did not hang around in the narrow hallway to visit.   Nobody really knew Hamilton. He never attended any floor dinners or meetings. He didn't go to the Wednesday happy hour or the occasional pot luck. He was seldom seen in the Plaza restaurant or the deli. He didn't attend the Saturday morning breakfast forums or the Friday evening live music performances. He was never seen at the Saturday or Sunday movies. The only time he seemed to emerge from his apartment was to pick up the mail and then he spoke to no one. Didn't he like people? Was he naturally asocial?

At his retirement party Detective Casey had sat at the table with Fox and told stories about the Rose Plaza. At one time there had been a wise guy, as the mob called their old timers, who was hidden at the Rose Plaza by WITSEC, the Witness Protection Program, but blew his cover and got bumped off.

Was Hamilton one of those?

There had been cases of WITSEC placing too many of its charges in the same town. That had happened in Orange County, California. Trouble was, those ex-mobsters had similar tastes and tended to congregate in the same sort of restaurant for breakfast where they soon recognized each other. They resorted to their old ways, got arrested again, and the local politicians protested to WITSEC management. Orange County was not to be a depository for old crooks in hiding.

Had WITSEC decided the Rose Plaza was a good place to stash their charges? Was Hamilton an ex-con in hiding? Or was he just a hermit who didn't like people?

If so, why?

Whatever or whoever it was, if Hamilton was under WITSEC maybe he blew his cover and his old enemies caught up with him.

Detective Fox could not imagine any of those elderly folks at the Rose Plaza committing grisly murder. Old ladies with criminal intent tended to use poison. They didn't slash throats, but you never could be sure. The world was full of crazy, angry, frustrated people. Some of them were elderly.

Some were cops.

Chapter three

Detective Fox returned to the twelfth floor, this time taking the freight elevator which was just south of the administrative offices. He had seen the surveillance cameras by the pair of elevators off the main lobby and the cameras inside those elevators as well. The freight elevator, however, had none, nor was there one in the ceiling outside the freight elevator at the twelfth floor. If someone wanted to get up there without being noticed by the security guard at the front desk, the freight elevator was the best bet. It was only a few yards away from Hamilton's apartment at the end of that short leg of the hallway. Hamilton might have chosen the location for its seclusion, but it also made it easier for his assailant to enter with the smallest chance of being observed.

Fox didn't think any of the residents of the twelfth floor were likely to be killers. His guess was that whoever cut Hamilton came from outside.

Intuition aside, his next task was to inform Major Hamilton's son Arthur. He had the emergency phone number in Syracuse, New York. It was now nine o'clock in the morning in Portland which meant Arthur Hamilton might be at lunch. Whatever.

Using his Portland police cell phone, Fox dialed the Syracuse number. All he got was a request to leave a voice mail message. Not confident that a voice mail message would imprint on the memory, Fox sent a text. "Please call Detective Fox, Portland Police, for an urgent message." It wouldn't do to send something as blunt as "Your father has been murdered." A text statement of regret did not have the same empathy as a speaker's tone of voice.

If would be even better if he could Skype. His police phone didn't have that app.

There was another emergency number, the lawyer and executor of Hamilton's estate. That was Evram Frizbee.

Frizbee was out, too. Maybe he slept in, or had a late breakfast. Fox had a personal rule: don't interrupt someone at their meal. Disturbing a bear or a lion at their feast could be a fatal error. Certainly people wanted to enjoy their food.

Fox wanted to enjoy his, too. He enjoyed Chinese food and had a favorite restaurant, Fongs, with a lunch special. It was close to the Chinese garden in Old Town, not far from the precinct station. This was authentic, where the Chinese ate and Mandarin was the only language heard. The waitress hardly knew any English at all.

Fox had suspected that the staff at Fong's were in the category of immigrants who were working at poor wages to pay off the cost of their transportation from China. For all he knew, they might actually live on the premises, like some sweat shop virtual prisoners. Immigration violations were not his department. As long as there was no prostitution or drugs Fox had no inclination to meddle. Portland had far worse criminal behavior to deal with. Even so, cultivating Mr. Fong could be an entree to issues he did have an interest in. A detective depended on having willing informants on the street.

Since Fox was obviously not Chinese no one was likely to intrude on his meal. He was a regular who always took a table at the rear of the restaurant with a view of the front entrance. Mr. Fong also knew he was a policeman, but his live and let live attitude said he was not a threat to the business. At least not for now. You never knew what might come up.

He needed a break from the nearly overwhelming challenge of the Hamilton murder. There was so much to investigate he felt inadequate. It was bad enough being accepted as a man. He also had to be accepted as a detective. He tried to escape into his Chinese lunch. Fox had difficulty enjoying his seafood special, shrimp, scallops, calamari, and something he couldn't identity, with a side of fried rice punctuated with little cubs of carrot and shreds of egg.. He was preoccupied with the grim image of Major Hamilton. The victim's eyes had been open and the expression on the dead face one of fear shock, anguish. Fox should just eat his lunch and not stare at the file Mrs. Grafton had given him.

He was building a case file. Besides listing the next of kin and the name of the executor of Major Hamilton's estate, there was a brief bio, the sort that might be posted verbatim when his picture was displayed as a new resident. Major Hamilton was a Vietnam War veteran, had gone to West Point, was decorated for bravery and wounded.

It didn't mention the extent of his injuries or how he had got them. If that was pertinent to the investigation Fox might get the man's medical records from the VA hospital. Was he disabled, for instance? To what degree? Was his discharge for medical reasons, or did he resign his commission when his tour of duty was up? Did he have PTSD?

Caryl Fox was not familiar with Post Traumatic Stress Disorder, what they called shell shock in World War I. He had learned that many Iraq War vets had committed suicide. Of course, most of those suicides were by firearm. Those victims didn't cut out their livers and slit their throats. But PTSD, fear of crowds, of strangers, of IEDs, might be a good reason for Hamilton's withdrawal.

On the other hand, Hamilton did get out, as the thong underwear attested, or maybe it came to him. Just as the man's Spartan apartment revealed something of the man himself, other factors like his web surfing habits and emails would possibly lead to his killer. Fox felt convinced it wasn't one of his feeble twelfth floor neighbors. There were lots of questions to be answered.

Anything that might be a clue to the man's character might be helpful in solving his murder. Everyone has a potentially fatal flaw. What was Hamilton's?

Mr. Fong had noticed that Fox wasn't eating. He came up quietly, concerned. "Is everything all right, Detective Fox?"

Fox looked up. "Just fine, Mr. Fong. I have a problem with a murder."

Before Fong could give a follow-up question Fox added, "You will probably read something about it in the Oregonian. They are always interested in crime stories. That and sports."

"If your lunch is not satisfactory, Detective. I can offer an almond cake for dessert, on the house."

"No thanks." It wasn't that Fox didn't like almond cake. He did. He just didn't want any favors, however kind, that might invite a payback later.

An almond cake would be a departure from his usual baked goods. His apartment in Multnomah Village was above a bakery. The landlord owner sometimes gave him a box of pastries to take to the precinct. When Fox went home after work it was to an apartment that smelled like bread, cakes, and pastries. Satiated by the fragrances he didn't need to eat much of it.

He did have a question for Mr. Fong. "Do you know if the gentleman's club on a hundred and twenty-eighth and Division is still open? The one with the Vietnamese girls?"

"No. No Vietnamese." Fong said in a way that might be taken to mean he had nothing to do with the large Vietnamese population in Portland, or if the girls in the club were Vietnamese. Or Fong was fearful of the vicious gangs that were active around Gresham. Or Fong, being Chinese, still had historical prejudices. China had often been at war with Vietnam. No wonder they talked about the inscrutable Chinese.

Fox would have to find out for himself.

First, when lunch was over, he had to talk to Hamilton's lawyer. As for an almond cake, as a gesture to

Mr. Fong he bought one on the way out to save for his afternoon coffee beak.

Chapter four

While waiting for a call back from Arthur Hamilton
Detective Fox decided to see who would inherit Major
Hamilton's estate. If Hamilton was rich, there might be
an heir interested in a short cut to the money. He wanted
to see the lawyer executor. He preferred face to face
meetings. People who didn't want to talk on the phone
could simply hang up. The ambush interview method
caught them off guard. Once he showed his badge they
couldn't just run away.

In today's conditions of police under stress,
running away from the cops was interpreted as an
admission of guilt and could get you shot. More
important, in a face to face interview Fox could read the
tells in people's expressions, knew when they were lying
or being evasive. He had played enough poker to learn
that. It was a skill useful if you were a detective.

Parking the unmarked in a handicapped spot on the
street in front of the old Multnomah building Fox found
the directory and took the rather creaky elevator up to
the top floor.

The door to the law office of Frizbee and Cachum
needed a coat of varnish. The gold lettering on the glass
was chipped. Just as Fox was used to sizing up a crime
scene, he was also analytical about the appearance of an
office. Some only looked new and prosperous, but
rented furnishings and no staff to go with it could
portray a front. In the case of Frizbee and Cachum, the
furniture might have been bought used, a leather visitor's
couch that might once have been a sign of prosperous
integrity now spelled seedy. The few magazines on the
coffee table were Golf and Cigar Aficionado. There was
no receptionist.

The door to the inner office was open. There was only one desk and the man behind was tilted back in his chair, his feet on the old fashioned blotter. He had grey hair, past due for a haircut, and was either needing a shave or contemplating a beard. He sat up when Fox knocked.

"Are you Frizbee?"

"That's me." Said with hesitation, suspecting a process server.

"Where's Cachum?"

"Died five years ago."

"Maybe you should take his name off the door."

"Sentimental reasons. Who are you?"

"Detective Fox, Portland police." He showed his badge.

Frizbee's faced flashed a look of alarm, quickly extinguished. "What's up?"

"I believe that you are the lawyer for Major Hamilton of the Rose Plaza on Terwilliger Boulevard."

There was a hesitation. "Has Hamilton done something?"

"He died. Actually, he was murdered. They tell me you're his executor."

"Who is they?"

"The management at the Rose Plaza." Fox checked his notes "Mrs. Grafton."

"Murdered, you say?"

"Yes. I'm trying to get hold of his son, listed as next of kin to be notified in case of, er, death. I need to know who might profit from his death."

"That's in the will, of course," Frizbee began, but was interrupted by he irritating chirp of Fox's cell phone.

Conveniently, it was Hamilton's son responding to Fox's text message. "This is Hamilton, what's it about? I got a text saying I should call you."

"This is Detective Fox of the Portland police. I'm sorry to have to report that your father has been murdered."

"What? When?"

Fox thought it prudent to put the cell phone on speaker so the lawyer could listen in. He was obviously interested and needed to know what the victim's son had to say. "We don't have an exact time of death. Probably in the last forty-eight hours."

"Jeeze."

"Do you have any idea who might want to kill him? I don't think this was a robbery."

"Sorry, Detective, I can't help you. I haven't spoken to my father in a couple of years. We weren't on good terms."

"Can I ask why?"

"I'm afraid my father was what you'd call a hawk. An anachronism. Anti-communist. Always telling war stories."

"I thought veterans didn't like to talk about the war. I understand he was in Vietnam."

"Would you believe my dad loved it. The war in Vietnam was the most exciting part of his life. He was in Laos, too. He even kept a kill book with pictures of the Viet Kong he'd killed. Made me sick. I finally got fed up. I called him a war criminal and he hung up on me. We haven't spoken since."

Fox was trying to take notes while holding the phone "Uh huh." He hadn't found a photo album in the apartment. That was something worth pursuing. Considering all the so-called collateral damage he felt war itself was a crime against humanity.

Lawyer Frizbee interrupted. "What about funeral arrangements? Do you want a celebration of life? They do that stuff at the Rose Plaza."

Fox explained. "I'm at the law office of your father's executor."

"There's nothing I'd want to celebrate about my father's death. He told me once he just wanted to be planted in the national cemetery. Said the government would give him an honor guard and a flag."

"Do you plan to be there?"

"Give me time to think about it. Murdered?"

"Yes."

"Where was he, in some bar? Mugged on the street?"

"No. He was found in his apartment." Fox didn't want to go into the graphic details and changed the subject. "Someone will have to dispose of his personal effects and furniture."

"I don't want any of his stuff. They can give it all to Goodwill."

"Do you know if he had any enemies?" Fox might have added, "Aside from you." Patricide was a long shot. The son was in Syracuse and had no contact with his father. Families. Go figure.

Fox had seen some bad family relationships, parents who were so abusive that their kids ran away and got sucked into the sex trade.. His own parents had a difficult time coping with their daughter's transgender choice but they weren't hostile, just shocked. Arthur Hamilton was hostile and bitter.

"Enemies? Just Ho Chi Min, but that guy's dead. Maybe sixty million Southeast Asians.

Frizbee interrupted. "Major Hamilton was a Vietnam veteran."

"Yes, I know." Fox remembered the missing silver star medal from the Major's display. He continued. "I suggest you contact Mrs. Grafton at the Rose Plaza. When we've done with the crime scene they'll want the apartment vacated." He remembered the Mexican workers next door. "They seem to be under constant remodeling there for the next tenants."

"Yes. I was there the year my parents moved in before Mom died. The place is like a revolving door. You go in ambulatory and go out feet first."

Fox had no comment about that. Some people had an aversion to old people's homes, the sight of wheelchairs and walkers, and the smell of urine. "If you can think of anything you have my number." He rung off and shook his head. To Frizbee he commented,

"Sometimes you call the family and everybody goes into hysterics at the news. This guy doesn't give a shit."

Frizbee agreed. "I'm surprised the son didn't want to know right away what he'll inherit."

Murder as a short cut to an inheritance or a life insurance pay out wasn't that uncommon, except some people didn't know that if you killed someone you could not inherit. But the son was in Syracuse. It was not likely that he'd fly to Portland to kill his father. "There might be something in Hamilton's will that could give me a lead to his killer."

"I haven't looked at it since he prepared it years ago. Sorry I can't help you. I prefer to open it only in the presence of the heirs."

Fox was disappointed. It would have been better of the lawyer was an old friend of the major and could reveal something about the man. Did he have any enemies who would want him dead? Frizbee had no clue. "You think you can tell me the terms of the will?"

"Client privilege."

If was worth a try. Fox handed the lawyer his business card. "Let me know if you actually know something." As he turned to leave Fox suggested, "Maybe it's time to get some varnish on that door and change the sign."

Frizbee didn't agree. "A one man law office doesn't look like much. Leaving Cachum's name is a sort of memorial. Gives the place the dignity of a long continuity."

So Frizbee was sentimental and held onto links with the past. Fox could relate to that. He had to admit he still hung onto that strapless party dress he had worn before the change and before his mastectomy. Just a reminder. Major Hamilton had done the same, keeping his old uniform with all those service ribbons. Some people couldn't let go of old memories.

Next stop? The medical examiner. Major Hamilton had a Purple Heart. The scars on his body might tell more of his story. Maybe there was a tattoo.

Chapter five

Still looking for clues to Major Hamilton's possible killer, Caryl Fox went back to the Rose Plaza to search the twelfth floor apartment for that scrapbook of kills. All he found was an empty Coors beer can in the kitchen trash and bagged it as possible evidence.. It should have been picked up for possible fingerprints or DNA. The Portland police had nabbed one burglar who helped himself to a slug of orange juice and left DNA on the bottle.

No kill book. Finding an old album from the Vietnam War was Caryl's own morbid curiosity. He knew little about the war which ended before his time. A kill book? Caryl's job wasn't to find out who Hamilton might have killed years ago, but who killed him last weekend.. The Vietnam War was a long time ago. Fox needed something current.

That didn't mean that victims of PTSD were not still haunted by their terrifying experiences. Maybe the VA medical records would have something. Had Hamilton been treated for PTSD? Was he part of a support group? Veterans of the Iraq and Afghanistan wars did sometimes lash out at family members, but usually it was suicide. If Hamilton did have PTSD something might trigger an old bad experience. Could be a sound or a smell. You never knew. But Hamilton's death was no suicide. You didn't cut out your own liver and then slit your throat while handcuffed to a chair.

It might be handy if Hamilton had a diary. No such luck. But we leave a trail wherever we go and whatever we do. The first place to look was the victim's cell phone for his list of contacts. Who called Hamilton and who did he call?

Surprisingly, Arthur Hamilton's number was not in his father's cell phone directory. Nor was his lawyer, but then his lawyer said he hadn't heard from Hamilton since he made out his will. As for the son, they hadn't been in touch for a long time, either.

Besides not associating with any of the Rose Plaza neighbors or residents, Major Hamilton also hardly called anybody.

Who called him? Caller ID left a trail, too. Fox went down the list. There were some "unidentified caller" numbers and several 800 numbers, possibly robo calls. This would take time.

Then there was Hamilton's PC, an obsolete model from Compaq. Of course, by the time a computer gets into the stores it is already obsolete. The latest models needed no password, just the fingerprint of the owner or maybe a voice recognition program responding to the cue chosen by the owner. Fox turned on the old Compaq but though it booted up as Windows ME, an obsolete operating system that Microsoft had long since abandoned, he couldn't get in. He needed the password. One of the police experts might be able to get around the password, but that wasn't Fox's expertise.

If he could break into that computer the cookies would lead him to the web sites where Hamilton was registered. The detective knew there were some lazy passwords, dumb ones like qwert. He consulted the DD214. Fox tried the Major's birthday. No luck. Maybe the date of discharge from the Army would be a good password. It didn't work either, nor did his date of enlistment.

It would be stupid to use your social security number as a password, because hackers could find that pretty easily.

Fox rummaged in Major Hamilton's desk drawer. There were a few bits of junk: a six inch ruler with an insurance company logo. Nail clippers, a plastic comb with some broken teeth, a letter opener carved from ivory, a little plastic envelope with an ugly looking wisdom tooth, a spent bullet, a pair of tarnished steel dog tags dated 1942. Dana Hamilton. Religion C, blood type B. That might have been Major Aaron Hamilton's father. So they were a military family. In spite of being otherwise pristine, Hamilton did keep some mementos.

Dana Hamilton's military ID number was not the same as the social security ID number. Could that be Hamilton's computer password? Using his father's number might be a sentimental link to the past.

Thoughts of military induction brought back his own bad memories. At the time Caryl Fox enlisted the military simply used social security ID numbers. When still a woman he had enlisted to get the signing bonus and GI Bill for college expenses.

The old "don't ask don't tell" policy broke down. His company commander had denounced him as a lesbian. Homosexuals were OUT. That was before the rules were changed. Now you could be in the military and be of any sexual preference. Even the chief of the army appointed by President Obama was openly gay.

Fox wasn't a lesbian. He just wanted to be a man. To be transferred to a male unit invited abuse and assault. Nobody wanted him in a gang shower. There was no place in the military for a transgender person. So much for that potential career. Too bad the VA would not spring for the cost of the sex change operations.

On a hunch Fox used the Major's father's military ID number as a password. First he tried the entire number. No luck. Then the last eight digits. He was in! Keeping his father's old World War II dog tags was a means of remembering the log on information.

He turned on Internet Explorer. What web sites had the Major visited? Fox got a surprise. Besides visiting Amazon, Major Hamilton had visited something called "Hot Asian Girls." That might explain the thong underwear with a little flower over the clit.

OK. There was even a Hot Asian Girl named Lotus. Could be a fake. Could be anywhere in the cyberspace world.

It was weird. If he kept pictures of his kills in Vietnam, why did he have a taste for Hot Asian Girls? The major was one twisted guy.

What else could he find out about the dead veteran? Your library reveals your interests in books. The Major's literary tastes, from the few books on his shelf, were military history, no surprises there, and a few memoirs of the Vietnam war, but no scrapbook of kills. There were no letters stuck between the pages as mementos or bookmarks.

The metadata collected off the internet, credit card purchases, and even the foods bought at Fred Meyer reveal more about a person than a few books on a shelf. Fox had made a game of speculating about people in the grocery checkout. Some lived on junk food. People on SNAP food coupons often picked unhealthy stuff. Maybe the reason they were poor was because they didn't know how to cook.

When Fox was kicked out of the army and was broke and nearly homeless he learned you could easily live a week on a chicken, the cheapest meat. Major Hamilton's refrigerator had packaged processed meats and the freezer contained prepared dinners from Trader Joes. One thing certain, the Major had not been a vegetarian.

Nor was he a teetotaler. His liquor cabinet had half a bottle of single malt Scotch.

Lotus might not even be real, a pseudonym for some chat site. Lotus might even be a digital fake used in a sting operation to trap pedophiles. That had been done before, an animated avatar of a twelve year old Asian girl. If Fox could find a real girl and her fingerprints were in the apartment, that would place her at the scene of the crime. But when?

Maybe the Major had a picture on his cell phone.

Bingo! He did.

There was a selfie with the major grinning and a dark skinned Asian girl who looked embarrassed. She did not want her face in that picture. Was she under age? It was hard to tell.

She apparently hadn't been shy about other pictures on the major's phone, intimate close-ups of private parts. She had a little dragon tattoo on her pudenda. If her name was Lotus, why not a flower tattoo? Or didn't it matter? So who was it?

Caryl reviewed the Major's computer file of "hot Asian girls." There were several named Lotus, which was a common name for a girl. There was no number on his cell phone call list with that identification. He had no clue to the real identity.

There didn't have to be any correlation to the computer file and the picture on the cell phone. He sent the selfie and the dragon tattoo shot to his own email address. He would print them out at the precinct. He was going to have to scour the gentlemen's clubs for Asian strippers and a pole dancer called Lotus. Maybe he'd get lucky.

All this told Fox a lot more about the reclusive Major Hamilton. Dirty old man? Fox wasn't ready to judge. He had seen plenty of johns while on the vice squad. That experience suggested that all men were letches. Some were lawyers, priests, even judges. The exposure by hackers of the wannabe adulterers web site covered the whole spectrum of men.

Well, Caryl was a man now, and had no such inclinations. To his mind, there were lots of creeps out there and some wore clerical collars. It was hard not to become cynical. He was sick of the flourishing sex trade in Portland. All those thirteen year old runaways who got drawn into prostitution their first month on the street.

Cynical or not Caryl had finally been so turned off by the work on the vice squad that investigating murders was preferable. It was usually simple. Someone got drunk and mad and had a gun. How many were a mere six pack from a life sentence? In most cases, killings were done by people you knew, spouses, relatives, neighbors, and the police knew from the start who did it. It was the random shootings in the aptly named Killingworth neighborhood that were hard to solve.

Fully thirty percent of murders were in fact never solved. The perps tended to be repeaters and eventually got busted for something else and didn't get charged until, years later, they bragged to a cell mate how they'd killed someone.

Detective Fox figured that the Asian girl would lead him to the killer if she wasn't guilty herself. He just had to find her. Shouldn't be hard, just tedious.

He tried the phone number on the Major's cell phone directory. No answer. If he left a text message, "Please call Detective Caryl Fox" and Lotus was the killer, that would tip her off. Better trace the address and make a surprise visit.

The tough part was putting together a case that the prosecutor would take to court. With luck they'd get a confession or a plea bargain and save the county the court costs. The courts were too backed up as it was. The constitution guaranteed a fair and speedy trial. If an accused couldn't make bail, they could languish in jail for many months only to be acquitted in the end.

Fox would find the girl called Lotus and go from there.

In the meantime, he wanted to see the medical examiner's report.

Chapter Six

When Caryl Fox got back to the precinct, the medical examiner's preliminary report was already on his computer. It was brief, the kind of shorthand you get from a form with blanks to fill out. Time of death was about forty-eight hours earlier, Saturday or possibly Friday night.

Compared with the cryptic impersonality of the report form, the digital photos were disturbingly graphic. They showed the major's body ready for autopsy, cleaned up but showing the open gash in his chest where part of his liver had been cut out, and the slit throat which had been cut with a single stroke, not hacked.

There were other wounds, old ones, scars from an appendix operation, an indentation on the left side which might be an old bullet wound. That might explain the Purple Heart medal he had displayed on his apartment wall. Unlike some veterans, Hamilton had no tattoos, no embarrassing souvenirs from a drunken night in Saigon or Hong Kong. For a sixty-seven year old, he was in pretty good shape, except dead.

Fox wanted to know more from the medical examination and telephoned. "This is Caryl Fox in Homicide. I got the report on Major Hamilton. What else can you tell me about it? I mean, did he put up a struggle?

"If he did it was short. His windpipe was crushed, the kind of thing from a karate blow. It wasn't enough to kill him but he'd have been pretty well incapacitated. I'd say he was taken by surprise."

So, a martial arts blow. That didn't strike Fox as something a little Asian girl could do, but you never knew. Some of those gals were tough and trained.

Fox tried to reconstruct. When he'd got to the apartment there was so much blood he didn't notice the wind pipe. That was obscured by the cut across the throat So he was hit in the throat, then taped to his chair and his throat cut. "I don't get the cut on his chest. What came first?"

"Obviously the chest was cut first. There was plenty of blood. If his throat was cut first he would have been already dead., the chest wouldn't have bled. Dead men don't bleed."

"Then why cut him again?" Victims of stabbings usually had multiple injuries caused by a frenzy of anger. This looked methodical and deliberate.

The medical examiner agreed. ":Looks to me like the prep cut out part of the man's liver so the victim was conscious and could see it happening. I've heard of it before. You cut out the victim's liver and eat it while he watches. It's a ritual murder."

"Ritual murder? That's sick."

"These are not nice people, Detective. The object is not just to kill, but to make the victim aware and suffer."

Fox hadn't heard of ritual murder.

The medical examiner continued. "It's a form of cannibalism. You eat the organs of your enemy and gain some of his power It's an ancient practice. In New Guinea the natives used to eat the brains of the dead. It's a ritual."

"That's sick."

The medical examiner laughed. "You must not be a Catholic. Didn't you ever take Communion? Drinking the blood and eating the body of Christ to gain salvation? "

"But that's symbolic."

"It's just one step removed from the real thing. The human race is primitive and barbaric."

"So do you think Major Hamilton's killer actually ate part of his liver?"

"You didn't find any piece lying around at the crime scene, did you?"

"No." Fox couldn't believe it "Maybe a piece was just taken as a souvenir."

"If that makes you feel better, you can believe that."

"Thanks."

"Just be thankful he wasn't killed by a Bedouin. You know what they do?"

"Should I ask?"

"They castrate the victim and choke him to death with his own testicles. Then they cut off his dick and stuff it in his navel, which makes him a kind of symbolic motherfucker. What do you think of that?"

Caryl Fox had neither testicles nor a penis. He had hormones for the sex change and facial hair, but there were limits. He hadn't thought it was actually an advantage not to have those private parts. At least, if you were threatened by a Bedouin with a knife.

What he needed to find out was what people in Portland's multicultural mix of immigrants would commit ritual murder?

Still reeling from the medical examiner's report, he accessed the major's phone, sent the photos to his own computer and printed out several 8x10 prints of Hamilton's selfie and the shot of the girl's pussy with the dragon tattoo. Then he got out his map of Portland and marked the locations of the gentlemen's clubs. Which ones might have girls who wore trade mark thongs like the one found under the Major's bed? Were any of them karate experts? With knives and a taste for human liver?

Fox also would have to ask Mrs. Grafton, the woman at the Rose Plaza, for the CCT records of all those surveillance cameras for that period of time to see who came into the building. He did not believe the killer was a resident but you never knew. The Rose Plaza had almost three hundred and fifty elderly residents, mostly women, of course. Interviewing every one of them would upset Mrs. Grafton. She obviously didn't want to cause a panic.

Fox could imagine that busybody Mrs. Seller cranking up the gossip engine. That was bad enough.

When the newspapers got hold of the story it might affect the ability of the Plaza to sell the apartments. No one would want to move into a place where people got their throats cut and their livers eaten while they were alive. No doubt.

Too bad the key fobs didn't record leavings, only entrances.

When he first came into the building he was asked to register at the front desk. Visitors were supposed to wear a sticker identifying them as guests, but his badge had been enough to justify his presence as a stranger at the Rose Plaza. Security was tight, but was it fool proof? He'd noticed the ceiling cameras by the elevator at the lobby, and even inside the elevator, but were they monitored, or just dummies to intimidate people? When he left the twelfth floor he went down the freight elevator only a few feet from Hamilton's apartment. There was no camera in that elevator and not in the ceiling of that hallway. Whoever had come in might not have been caught by the CCT system.

There had been no answer to his text message to the number identified on the Major's cell phone as Lotus. If Lotus had caller ID and saw the call came from the police, she might have good reason not to reply. Well, there were other possibilities and he had to pursue all of them. He was well aware that he was not accepted by the gay or lesbian community and treated like a freak in the police department. He simply must not fail with this case.

Armed with the selfie photograph, Fox began his methodical search of locales where an Asian girl might wear a thong with a little flower on the front.

Chapter seven

Besides a Starbucks on nearly every corner and over two hundred food carts, Portland, Oregon had about two hundred nude dancing locales. From his time on the vice squad, Fox figured the best place to start his search for the girl called Lotus was on the east side of the Willamette. As housing had grown scarce and expensive, new immigrants and the working poor had moved to the limits of the urban growth boundary of the city, from 82nd street, also known as hookers' alley, east to Gresham near the end of the light rail line.

That's where there were pockets of Vietnamese, Africans, Russians, and eastern Europeans. That's where the under funded schools, burdened by students who knew little English, had a graduation rate of under 50%. More than ten percent of the children in Portland were in poverty. Hungry kids don't learn well. Those that did go to school were sometimes sent home with food on Fridays so they would have something to eat over the weekend. For them summer vacations were a time of hunger.

Forty percent of the kids in school lived with only one parent. No surprise that some kids ran away and lived on the streets until pimped by one of the sexual predators.

Caryl Fox didn't wear a uniform, which could be a disadvantage if you wanted people to talk to you, and he drove an unmarked car. Even so, the radio antennas in the roof could be a giveaway.

Portland was generally friendly to the LGT community. Portland State University had unisex bathrooms. Even so, not everyone was tolerant. If Caryl Fox were spotted as transgender, there might be a confrontation. At first he had found it awkward to choose a wardrobe that was manly but not affected. You didn't have to wear cammies to be manly. Besides, camouflage clothes brought back bad memories of his military service.

It wasn't unusual to find cross dressers on the Tri-Met transportation system. It wasn't difficult to pick out the gay men or the dykes. So what? Being transgender was no crime. He was just different, and that should be OK in Portland. Most of the time.

Detective Fox began his combing of the nude dancing locales at 82nd Street and Foster Road. They were easy to spot: windowless buildings painted an ugly purple. Though there were signs advertising nude girls, the owners were sensitive to the outcries of some neighborhood associations.

Fox parked in the lot next to the first club and went inside. The place was dark except for the stage and the pole. Unless they wanted to be ringside for a lap dance, most men in the audience stayed in the shadows, probably so they could jerk off.

The bouncer recognized him. "Carol Fox. Haven't seen you in awhile." He was a short, stocky guy who wasn't intimidating except for the firearm he wore conspicuously on his belt. "You still on the vice squad? This a friendly visit or are you slumming?" He gestured toward the naked dancer who was doing something gymnastic on the pole. "We got nothing to hide. She don't, anyway."

Fox ignored the quips. "It's Caryl now, not Carol. I moved up to homicide for a better class of creeps. Right now I'm looking for a girl." He took a copy of the selfie from his folder of photographs. "You know her?"

The bouncer moved into a better light and studied the face. "The boss doesn't hire Asians."

"What about the guy with her?"

"Never saw him. What is he, a pimp?"

Fox shook his head. "Someone cut out his liver and ate it whiled he watched."

The bouncer swallowed hard like he might have puked. "Couldn' be me. I'm a vegetarian."

"I avoid organ meats myself," Fox admitted. "What about this tattoo?" He showed the dragon pudenda.

The bounder smirked. "Nice work if you can get it. No. Haven't seen that one. I've seen plenty. Nice dragon."

"What about the guy? Retired Major. Vietnam."

"Looks like he got a taste for Vietnamese pussy."

Fox nodded. "Would you mind posting this someplace? Ask the girls who work here if they've seen her. The name we have is just Lotus."

The bouncer shook his head. "They don't use their real names here. We got a lot of turnover. They don't last long, move onto better jobs. I think some have this fantasy of finding a husband."

"Not likely."

"Would you believe we get a lot of college girls in here? They think it's a kick, showing off their titties.

"Takes all kinds."

Fox had also taken a shot of the thong underwear with his phone and showed the picture. "Seen underwear like this?"

"The flower's a nice touch, but some of the girls who do wear these like sequins for the glitter."

Seeing only a handful of customers lurking in the shadows, Fox commented, "Quiet today."

"Come back later, Caryl. I heard you did the change.

"Does it matter?"

"To each her own, or his own. Whatever."

Before he left Fox warned, "I hope you got a carry permit for that piece."

"Hey, this is my home. I got a cot in the back room."

"I bet you rent it by the hour."

"Would you believe? Boss doesn't approve of me making something on the side."

"I bet he goes to church on Sunday, too."

"Saturday."

So was the owner a Jew or a Seventh Day Adventist? Fox didn't ask. He left the gloom of the gentleman's club and went out into the welcome sunlight of the parking lot. A couple of kids who should have been in school were hanging around his unmarked. They had noticed the license plate.

"You kids gotta be over eighteen to go in there," he warned, then added. "And it's only for gentlemen."

He started the engine and fired up the GPS. Where was the nearest next one? He had entered several addresses for the day's search. Hundred and twenty-eighth and Division. He might have better luck there

Chapter eight

The next club could have been a twin of the first, except this one catered to the Russian crowd. The girl on the pole was a leggy blonde with a pony tail and a sports bra. She was obviously in it for the use of the pole for training purposes in the hopes that pole dancing would develop into an Olympic sport.

Caryl had to admire the athleticism and was watching when the owner approached him. He was a Russian with dark curly hair, a heavy beard, and a leather vest, no gun. If Fox had known Rasputin he could have thought the Russian was an impersonator. He didn't look like he needed a gun.

"You like lap dance?"

Fox showed his badge. "Not today. I'm not with vice any more. Trying to track down a girl who might be involved in a murder." He took out one of the 8 by 10s. "Goes by the name of Lotus. Ever seen her?"

"No Chinese girls here. Only Ukrainians."

"Everybody's got a specialty. What about the man in the picture with her?"

The Russian studied the picture carefully. "Might have. I think he was in here a while back. Didn't just come for show. Shopping for girl."

"Looks like he moved on to Asians."

"So who is he?"

Fox cocked his head. "He's the victim. Someone cut his throat." He didn't want to mention the liver again.

"The girl?"

"Maybe. I need to find her."

"I put up the picture. Maybe someone know her."

"Know a club that hires Asian girls?"

The owner rubbed his grizzled cheek. "Try the place on Interstate. Is new."

"Thanks." Fox used his only word of Russian. "Dosvidanya."

This was going to take a long time.

Even if he did find the right club, the girl might have moved on to another or retired to something more savory.

He drove up Interstate Avenue following the Yellow Max line that terminated at Expo Center. He found the joint. In the nearly deserted parking lot one of the girls was sitting in the sun in a robe outside the back door and taking a cigarette break. She was a bleached blonde with dark roots that needed touching up. She looked tired and burnt out.

He walked up to her, showing his badge. "Maybe you can help me. I'm detective Fox investigating a murder. Have you ever seen this girl?"

"Maybe."

"What about the guy beside her?"

"Yeh. " She frowned. "A creep. 'Course they're all creeps."

"Must be hard to keep smiling at them."

"I'm a good actress. I'm trying out for a part in Grimm." Grimm was a TV series filmed in Portland and featuring various monsters like the German fairy tales.

"Well, this creep was pretty grim. Somebody cut his throat."

"He probably deserved it."

"Did you know his name?"

She shook her head. "Only saw him once. Wanted a lap dance. Asked for my phone number. Against the rules here."

Fox was about to go inside the club when his cell phone twittered. "Yeh? Fox here."

"This is the medical examiner. Got another detail for you."

"Shoot."

"Guess what we found in the Major's throat?"

"What?" Fox remembered the story of the Bedouins. "His balls?"

"His Silver Star medal."

"Makes sense." Fox remembered framed citation and the display on the Major's wall, the spot where the medal was missing. "This has to have something to do with his military history. He served in Vietnam, got himself an Asian, probably Vietnamese immigrant girl friend."

"Found the girl yet?"

"I'm looking." Fox clicked off but before he could put the phone back in his pocket it rang again..

It was a reporter from the Portland Tribune, the free twice a week newspaper that sometimes beat the Oregonian to the best stories.. "I'm calling about the murder at the Rose Plaza."

"How'd you find out?"

"Got a scanner in my car."

"I can't give you details other than he was found dead in his apartment on the twelfth floor."

"Got a suspect yet?"

"I'm looking for a person of interest. Maybe you can run a photo with your story. Got a selfie of the victim and his girl friend known only as Lotus. You on a cell phone?"

"Sure."

"I'm sending their photo to you now. The victim is a retired Major, Aaron Hamilton. War hero of the Vietnam war. Got a Silver Star medal for bravery." Fox didn't mention that the medal was found in the victim's throat.

"Any more details?"

"Can't tell you that. Don't want any copycats running around Portland knocking off Vietnam vets. Those guys have enough to worry about." It was bad enough that some came home with PTSD only to be spat on as baby killers. The war might be over but the nightmares lingered on and on.

There was a pause. "Thanks for the picture. Got any more?"

"Nothing you could run in a family newspaper."

End of conversation. If the Tribune did run the photo of the Major and Lotus that might save Fox the trouble of hitting all the nude joints. It might also warn the entire population of the city that he was looking for Lotus. That could put her in danger.

Lotus was just a possible lead in the case. She might just be a coincidence. He decided to go back to the crime scene for another look.

Chapter nine

By now the entire Rose Plaza was buzzing with the story of the twelfth floor murder. What else did those mostly old ladies have to gossip about? Detective Fox could just imagine that Mrs. Seller on the phone and knocking on doors. Maybe he should recruit her as an informant. While ruminating on that idea he used Hamilton's fob to get into the first floor administrative offices to revisit Mrs. Grafton.

She was not happy when he asked for a copy of the CCT recordings starting the Friday before until Monday morning when the body was discovered. The word was out about the murder and as official gatekeeper her desk was the first target of reporters. She had anticipated his arrival and had her excuse ready.. "If you want to see the tapes of all the main entrances and elevators you'll have to see Arlan our IT manager. He can also get you the footage for the wellness center and the swimming pool, but I doubt if those would be any help."

"Thanks." Fox added them to his folder of photos. "I noticed that there's no camera by the freight elevator."

She sighed with the frustration and stress the incident had brought down on her head. "You'll have to talk to Arlan, he maintains the security system. If you have criticism of his system you'll need to be diplomatic. He can be thin skinned."

"Thanks for the warning."

"You might also check with the security guard. There's always someone on duty. Twenty-four hours."

"One guard? Is he always at the front desk?"

Ms. Grafton could see the flaw Fox was after. "He makes the rounds of the parking lot several times a night. We've had some car prowls."

"Does he also walk the hallways?"

Mrs. Grafton shook her head. Her frustration and growing irritation was palpable. "The Plaza is four blocks long, including the Heights wing. The Tower is twelve stories. We have miles of corridors here. He'd be pacing the halls all night."

"So the night watchman relies on the monitors." Fox had noticed the bank of monitors at the front desk.

"It's usually quiet here. No all night wild parties. Our residents tend to go to bed early."

And see nothing, Fox thought. "Maybe I could talk to the night watchman. Got a name and number?"

"It's not always the same person. We contract for the security. You'll have to call them to find out who was on duty." She looked up the number and gave it to him.

"Thanks. I'll do that." Fox was still reasonably certain that a resident would be unlikely to cut the major's throat and certainly not take a chunk of his liver. If this were a HUD low income housing building with psychos, drunks and addicts, he could expect violence. But here? Unlikely. The Rose Plaza was a respectable, quiet residence.

Fox had already seen the maid, Mrs. Alvarez. "What about the employees? This could have been a staff member."

Now Mrs. Grafton was defensive. "We have over a hundred and eighty on staff, Detective. All have been vetted."

"Which means you did a background check."

"Right."

"Are they also fingerprinted?"

"Not normally." She was now nervously fiddling with a ball point pen. "The new immigrants would have their fingerprints on file with Immigration. We don't require that."

Fox thought, if this Lotus gal isn't born in the United States, maybe her fingerprints found in the apartment will identify her. He doubted if there would be DNA filed that would match pubic hairs or excretions in the thong underwear, if there were any. His experience in

Vice told him girls in that business tended to have their privates shaved. Fox checked his pocket notebook. "Mrs. Alvarez is Cuban, right?"

"Yes, she is. Our service jobs are often filled by foreigners. We have Russians, Cubans, Philippines, Africans. When you are a new immigrant this is a place you can find a job until your English is up to speed."

"And your skills."

"We do train people. Sometimes, I'm sorry to say too often, they come here, get training, then move to a place that pays more. Some of our twenty-four hour care people are college students working part time. Same goes for the wait staff in the dining room. The night shift has some African Americans who hold several jobs."

That gave Fox a building full of suspects. "Could you get me a roster of who was on duty from Friday until Monday?"

Grafton was reluctant. "I'll have to ask the payroll clerk if she has time to do that for you."

'Swell." Fox turned to leave. "Oh, Major Hamilton was a Vietnam war vet. Do we have more veterans here at the Plaza?"

"Quite a few. They have a monthly lunch."

"Who's in charge? Maybe he can help me."

"Or she," Grafton corrected. "Quite a few of our women residents are veterans, too." Efficient as ever, she wrote down a name on a Post It note. "Mr. Cooper is in charge of that committee. Bill Cooper."

"Thanks. I'll ask him." He wrote the name in his pocket notebook.

Grafton pulled open a lower drawer. This one wasn't locked. "You'd better have a copy of our directory." She extracted a spiral bound book. "This will save you some time. Now is there anything else you need to know?" She was obviously keen on getting back to her own job.

"The location of the Major's storage locker. I have the key."

"Don't you need a search warrant for that?"

"Not when there's a murder and it's the victim's stuff."

It took longer for her to find that information, but she added it to the note she'd written with the vets' club name.

"Thank you for your help."

She didn't seem mollified.

He added, "You are very good at what you do."

That helped.

As he made his way to the breezeway that separated the front and rear parking lots Fox mumbled to himself. "Over three hundred residents, almost two hundred employees, many of the foreigners. Too bad this isn't a run of the mill domestic violence case. Husband gets drunk and wife shoots him. Cut and dried. Not this case."

The chief of detectives was not his friend. Maybe he got this case to be proven a failure.

Before he left the Rose Plaza he got directions from the front desk clerk on where to find the parking garage. The building was complicated. What was the third floor of the north end assisted living wing became the second floor of the so-called tower.

The parking garage, three floors, was below that.

By odd coincidence, Major Hamilton's parking space at the far north end of the garage was the same spot Casey had told his successor about. It was where another Rose Plaza murder had taken place. Unlucky? He approached the Audi cautiously, did a walk-around. Though not the latest model, it looked well maintained. No bumps or bruises.

He opened the driver's side and checked the glove box. Nothing but a pair of cheap sunglasses. The console had the car's maintenance log, registration, and an old Portland city map. There was nothing in the back seat. The Major had been tidy. No empty coffee cups on the floor, no trash.

The trunk had to be unlocked.

In the trunk the Major had kept some recyclable grocery bags from Fred Meyer. The jack was in its compartment. Hamilton had kept a spare quart of oil and some windshield washing fluid.

Pushing the grocery bags aside Fox lifted the cover that hid the spare tire. That was a favorite place for some drug smugglers to stash their wares. He found nothing but the spare. What did he expect? One never knew. A serial killer might carry a supply of duct tape, weapons, garbage bags for pieces of the victim, maybe even a GoPro camera for a souvenir video. Hamilton had not been into that.

It would be nice if the Audi, like some rental cars, carried a GPS that recorded wherever the car was driven and even at what speed. Some day they wouldn't need traffic cops. The car's GPS might automatically record and even report any incident of speeding or running a stop sign or red light. Nothing like being ratted out by your own car.

A better bet would be the storage locker. Now how did he get to that? He had the locker number.

It took a circuitous search to access the storage lockers. First he had to go back to the first floor and return to the lobby, then take one of the two small elevators down to the basement.

That, too, was a warren of hallways. There were over a hundred lockers down there, all identical. He finally found Hamilton's and the key fit.

The Major's storage locker had several cartons, a set of matched luggage, a duffle bag stuffed with camping gear.

One of the cartons contained old tax returns.

Finally, on a high shelf, Fox found what he was looking for. It was a flat box containing some family pictures in frames and a photo album. The pages were of a poor quality, not acid free and were brittle with age. Some of the pictures, held down with corner tabs, were loose. The photos, all black and white, needed no color to be gruesome.

This was Major Hamilton's kill book. They were all of Vietnamese and numbered. The light was poor in the storage locker catacombs, but Fox thought he could make out the details. A couple of shots showed the Major, then a grinning lieutenant, standing with a boot on the corpse of a Viet Kong in black pajamas like a big game hunter who just shot a lion. There were other pictures of a village being set afire and bodies of women and children on the ground. It looked to Fox, who had never seen combat in his brief service in the army, like the scene of an atrocity. Had Hamilton been at My Lai?

Just as the selfie photo had placed the Major and his Asian girl friend in the apartment, there might be more information in those photos. He put the album back in its box and took it with him.

He wandered through some wrong turns before he found his way out of the storage locker maze to the elevator. Before he could get to his car, Fox was cornered by a blonde girl pushing a Channel Eight microphone in his face. Why did all those women on TV have to be blonde? He had seen her before. She knew him from a sex trafficking case. "This is Detective Caryl Fox. What do you have to tell the audience of Channel Eight about this murder?"

Before answering, his glance caught the TV van with its antennas up and ready like an attentive dog's ears. "I can't comment on the details at this time." He held up the Plaza phone directly. "So far I have over three hundred potential suspects. Want to be on the list? Where were you between Friday night and Monday morning?"

Caught off guard, she actually blushed. Maybe he had hit a nerve, someplace she wasn't supposed to be, or with someone she didn't want anyone to know about.

He had his hands full with his folder, the box with the kill book, and the Plaza directory. Fox juggled one of the selfie pictures from his folder and held if up for the camera. "Here's a photo of the victim and a woman we have not identified. If anyone knows who she is, please call Detective Caryl Fox of the Portland police. That's all I have to say at this time."

He then ducked and tried to escape to his car which was inconveniently blocked by the TV truck.

He had cast a wide net. Considering what he had found on Hamilton's computer and cell phone, it was likely that he had met the girl called Lotus at one of those nude dancing joints. If the Portland Tribune and Channel 8 ran the selfie, Fox would be spared a door to door check of the scores of so-called gentlemen's clubs. Someone would come forward.

Lotus was his only lead.

He was convinced that the major's gruesome murder was not the work of a little Asian girl. Of course, he could be wrong. It might be coincidence, that there was no connection at all between Lotus and the killer.

He did think that the girl was a link. He thought of a number of possible scenarios. Maybe the girl had a boy friend, brother, or father who would teach Hamilton a fatal lesson for messing with Lotus.

Now to find out what fingerprints in the apartment would identify the killer. Too bad he or she didn't just leave the weapon behind with fingerprints and DNA. Solving these cases wasn't always easy. Unfortunately, of the ones that weren't, too many went unsolved, fully thirty percent, in fact. When all the leads dried up, people forgot.

Though since his transfer from Vice Fox had dealt with several killings, they were simple: typical late night shootings outside a bar in view of a CCT and witnesses. Witnesses testified. The DA got plea bargains that saved the cost of a jury trial. Better yet, twice the perp, cornered, decided to shoot it out or appear to threaten the police in a suicide by cop incident. Those cases were done.

This one was different. Caryl Fox wanted a win, not a cold case or a botched investigation that led to a mistrial. He wanted the satisfaction of presenting a solid case to the DA that would stand up in court and lead to a conviction. His role was only one step in the turning wheels of justice. Until the steel doors slammed on the killer there was no reason to celebrate.

Chapter ten

At the Central Precinct he had inherited Detective Casey's old office. That had required some sex trafficking cases be left behind for J.J., his successor at the East Side precinct station, while he picked up some of Casey's that were still pending, the ones whose leads had dried up. Those were there for him to pore over when he had time.

One odd case was the State of Oregon versus Ed Sutherland. It had also begun at the Rose Plaza and ended in a surprising acquittal.

The politics of the precinct had made the transition from Vice to Homicide awkward at times, for everyone knew he was transgender. There were some gay officers but even they didn't know what to make of him. Those who had known him as Carol had trouble with Caryl. There was tension over the inappropriateness of some jokes. For instance, if he leaned over the shoulder of someone at a computer station, he had to be careful not to touch them. A hand on a shoulder could be misinterpreted.

How lucky so-called normal people had it. You could argue, as some did, that being homosexual or transgender was just another form of normal, but in a way it was like religion. If you thought yours was the only way, anyone else was suspect or inferior or simply different. No doubt about it, Caryl was different.

He just wanted to be himself, however odd that was in the minds of some people. They should get over it so he could get on with his life and his job.

His hope was that they would just get used to him using the men's toilet where he had to sit down to pee.

You'd think that being transgender would made it easier to relate to the gay community. I wasn't. Some straights weren't accepting, either. To serve and protect was supposed to mean serving and protecting everybody, not just this or that privileged group like whites or straights.

As a transgender he wasn't accepted anywhere.

When he walked into a nude dancing club, before anyone would be able to question his transgender person, he'd simply show his badge and get down to business. He could tell people to get over it, but he had trouble himself. It was too late to change his mind. He had to put aside all those thoughts and pay attention to business.

For now that business was the fingerprints found in the twelfth floor apartment. So far the only ones were Major Hamilton's and one other set, presumably the mysterious Lotus. Those prints were in the bathroom and bedroom. They were also on a couple of wine glasses that had been put away in the dishwasher but not yet washed.

What about other prints? Caryl had noticed that the maid wore latex gloves. That was probably to protect her skin from harsh cleaning chemicals.

The Major had been taped into his office chair. It would be almost impossible to tear and apply that tape without leaving prints. As for DNA from secretions in the thong underwear, that lab was so backlogged it could take a couple of months.

To review what he had so far, Caryl Fox assembled his evidence on a standard whiteboard. There wee several views of the victim and shots of the apartment, the selfie, and several x-rated prints of the girl's private parts.

He was trying to reconstruct the Major's life, his habits, his movements, anything that might be a clue to his contacts.

The man's computer, brought back to the precinct, for study, had a file of nude Asian women, some of whom might be under age, but hard to classify as kiddy porn. Major Hamilton did look at porn. That wasn't illegal. OK, so he was a dirty old man, but if you bumped off everybody who ever looked at porn on the internet the population would be greatly diminished! Why was he killed and by whom?

So far Caryl's only solid lead was the girl called Lotus, if he could find her.

The list of numbers saved on Hamilton's I-phone might lead him to the girl, but didn't. Caryl realized that Hamilton had two phones--the cell and the hard wired one furnished by the Rose Plaza.

At five o'clock Detective Fox went back to his apartment upstairs of a bakery in Multnomah Village. The fragrance of baking bread and pastries had so permeated his apartment that his clothes sometimes smelled like yeast. An advantage was he never had to buy fresh bread. There were always surplus loaves he could take his pick of, thanks to his generous landlord.

He liked the funky neighborhood with its little shops and the Annie Bloom independent bookstore. Of course, like most densely populated parts of Portland, parking was a beast, but he had a spot reserved behind the store.

He walked a couple of blocks to Otto and Anita's little German restaurant for a wiener schnitzel and dill pickle soup. Except for lunches at his favorite Chinese place downtown, he seldom ate out, but he was tired and didn't feel like cooking. Cooking for one was a bore and he hated leftovers. Those take home boxes he sometimes brought home from Fong's Chinese restaurant ended up soggy or worse in the back of his refrigerator. .

Like many of his generation, he lived alone. It was nice if you could find a partner to share expenses but Caryl wasn't into a relationship. He was transgender, not a homosexual. Now that he was a guy women he might date thought he was too weird.

A dog might be a good companion, but they demanded maintenance, walks, carrying a bag of poop you then had to get rid of. A cat was easier to care for, but he didn't want to be servant to an aloof cat. His landlord, the baker, had a couple of cats to keep mice away. That was enough. He'd had a gold fish but he forgot to change the water and it died. Face it, he told himself, he was too preoccupied with his job to think of much else. Maybe he could buy a plant, a cactus that never needed water.

It added up to being essentially a lonely person wrapped up in his job which at the moment was the Hamilton murder.

The Hamilton murder was a puzzle. How could a killer get into the high security building without being noticed?

Maybe he was searching in the wrong place. Mrs. Grafton had said they had nearly two hundred on the staff. To interview every one of them would take time. Not only was there a large roster of employees, some on call. They also had a home help department, a valet service for parking, and remodelers.

Though the building had been built in the 1950's which marked it as old by American standards, every time someone died their apartment was stripped and remodeled to the specifications of the new member. The major's son would have one month to clear out the apartment. The remodel team would then move in with a new set of specifications.

Detective Fox had seen the two Mexican plasterers working across the hall from Hamilton's apartment. He'd already spoken with them. They didn't work on the weekend. It was on the weekend that the medical examiner had calculated was the time of death.

So nobody heard anything or saw anything. The victim sat dead while the flies responded to the smell of blood and death until the maid showed up on Monday. Studying the Plaza directory Fox saw that many residents lived alone. Most were widows. Fox imagined that one could easily die and not be discovered for days, alone in a big building with over three hundred residents and nearly two hundred on staff, but still alone.

That old Mrs. Seller said the Major was a recluse who didn't interact with anybody. What did she have? A team of snoops and gossips who knew everything and everybody? Did she also know that the retired Major patronized a nude dancing establishment and looked at Asian porn? Was Seller a voyeur watching a voyeur? Sick.

Fox knew that for criminals the most dangerous people were the old ladies who had nothing better to do than watch the neighborhood and little kids who were ignored and therefore invisible observers. You had to be cautious about what to believe. Sometimes the information they provided was embellished by fantasy.

Fox still had some lines to pursue. The veterans luncheon leader, for instance. So far all he had found out was what sort of person the major was, but that hadn't led to his killer. Finding the Asian girl was his main hope.

There had to be a motive for murder, even if it was the voices in the head of a psychopath. The Major had not been robbed. Maybe the girl called Lotus had a boy friend, a father, or an uncle who disapproved of her liaison with the old veteran.

It was raining the next morning, one of those incessant Portland rains that weren't heavy but persistent. This could go on for days.

On his way to the downtown precinct from Multnomah Village he stopped at the Rose Plaza. Mrs. Grafton had succeeded in persuading the IT manager to produce a couple of duplicate CCT records. At his office Carol ran through them, noting the frequent activity of cars coming and going in the Plaza breezeway. Radio Cab was the most frequently used company.

What Caryl was looking for was activity from Friday night to the following Sunday. The Major had been murdered in the last forty-eight hours. Who came and went?

CCT records showed people entering and leaving the front entrance at the breezeway. The street entrance at P1 which was used by staff and residents did not show Major Hamilton. How did he get into the complex? Apparently only through the garage door.

Just as a record was made of every fob use, the garage door opener did, too. So Hamilton came and went by his car. That got him into the garage and his fob was used to enter the building from there.

He did turn up in the CCT record of people entering the P3 level of the garage. That was confirmed by the record of his use of his garage door opener. To get from the garage into the building required the fob. That activity was well documented, but the camera by the electric entry door did not show any Asian girl. When Hamilton came and went he was alone.

If so how did she get into the building and leave her thong behind the Major's bed? At first Caryl thought maybe the thong was a souvenir from an encounter away from the Plaza. Maybe the fingerprints left behind weren't hers. Perhaps that line or reasoning was a dead end. But wait...

He studied the selfie on the white board. In the background he could just make out the corner of the Major's computer desk. She had been in the apartment. The selfie and the series of intimate photos were all date stamped. They had been taken very late Friday night. Wine glasses in the dishwasher and the photos added up to quite a party. So did Lotus kill him?

Oddly, there was no CCT record of the Asian girl at all. How did she get into the building? By what entrance? The mysterious Lotus had been in the apartment that weekend. If so, how did she get into the Rose Plaza without being noticed? When he had arrived at the front desk he'd been asked to sign in. Visitors were supposed to wear a sticker tag that said "visitor."

He'd better go over the sign in book. Even if he didn't know any name but "Lotus" whoever was the receptionist would remember that pretty, young Asian face.

Hamilton's credit card record would tell where he went and what he bought. Caryl would have to check that, too. His credit card record would tell where he went if he bought anything or ate in a restaurant if he charged his meal. Getting that record from the credit card company would involve some paperwork. If he charged drinks at a nude dancing place, that would be an easy trace, save Caryl a lot of driving around.e

The major's Visa and American Express cards were still in his wallet along with some cash, so robbery wasn't the motive.

The only thing missing at first glance was the Silver Star medal. There had been traces of blood on the plaque where it had been displayed, but no fingerprints. The medical examiner had found the medal in the Major's throat. Did the killer have something against veterans? Against veterans in general, or against the Major specifically?.

Caryl was about to call the credit card companies when his phone rang. It was Hal Savage, his old partner at the east Side precinct. "Hi, Caryl, how's life in homicide?"

"It's like studying for a term paper in grad school. Tedious."

"I've got news for you. The picture you circulated and was on the news last night? We've found your Asian girl."

Chapter eleven

"Did someone call in a tip?"

"Someone found her. She's dead. Some kids found the body up at Rocky Butte lookout. Strangled."

Rocky Butte had a view of the Columbia river and the I-205 bridge. It was a favorite spot for kids making out. It had to be closed after ten o'clock because there'd been a shooting there.

"Is the body still there?"

"It's pouring rain, Caryl. The medical examiner took it to the office in Clackamas."

"Strangled, you say?"

"Yep. Choked on her own panties."

"Sexual assault? Was she raped?"

"She was naked from the waist down. The medical examiner will be able to say if she was raped. Might get some DNA."

"I'd like to have a look at her. What about ID?"

"The perp was either careless or accommodating enough to leave her purse. Like they wanted people to know who she was and that she was dead. "

"Like a warning?"

"Could be."

"So what was in her purse? Money? Credit cards? What?"

"Driver's license. Name is Long Nguen. They even left her cell phone."

Caryl had Major Hamilton's phone. Phones had become a repository of a person's life, photos, videos, and contacts. "Great. I have to see if she called Hamilton with it. I bet her killer's number is on it, too."

"Can't. It's blocked. Encrypted."

The new phones were expensive, the monthly contracts, too. In the interests of privacy and security

Apple and other phone manufacturers had included blocking software. With the latest models only the owner could use the phone. Even the FBI and NSA couldn't get in. At least the girl's ID was in the purse. "So Hal, her name is Long Nguen?"

"Long. Long is Vietnamese for dragon."

"So did this victim have a dragon tattoo on her pussy?"

"How did you know?"

"Major Hamilton had some pictures on his camera."

"How convenient. You gonna send me a copy as an email attachment??"

"I don't know, Hal. You might be accused of keeping porn on the office computer."

"Evidence, Caryl. Just evidence."

"I'd better get up to Rocky Butte and see the crime scene, then run down to Clackamas. I haven't been at the medical examiner's since they moved."

"You'll have company. You'd better hook up with your old partner J.J."

"Hook up?" J.J. was the only Moslem on the vice squad and he the only transgender. They had worked together before as a team by default because nobody really wanted to work with a transsexual or a Moslem. The cops had their own prejudices.

Hal laughed. "I don't mean hook up in that way. Wouldn't want to pry into your sexual preferences, Caryl. This is no ordinary murder. We know this victim. She's a part time hooker. That makes this a case for vice."

Just when Fox was glad to get away from vice and the east side precinct, here he was again. Was this going to be part of a turf war? He had got along well enough working with J.J. as long as she restrained herself from telling politically incorrect jokes that hurt.

So, Lotus was the Asian girl's business name. She was really Long Nguen. He wrote it down. Now what was the quickest route to get to Rocky Butte?

Detective Fox had never been to Rocky Butte before and used his GPS to find it. It looked like a stone fortress. The retaining walls that held the parking lot in place resembled a castle, might have been built during the Depression as a WPA make work project.

When he got to Rocky Butte J.J. was waiting for him, sitting in a squad car at the edge of the narrow access road. Fox pulled up in front of her. He got out and walked back.

She rolled down her window and said, "You took your time."

"Never been up here before. How you been?"

She was in civilian clothes, her hair hidden for modesty under a sort of turban. She wore no makeup and didn't need it. Caryl envied her good looks. As a woman he had never been attractive.

One of the benefits of being a man was you didn't have to fuss with how you looked. You didn't have to hide behind makeup or sell yourself. He had always hated society's emphasis on how women looked. It hearkened back to the slave trade, women as chattel. A man could just be himself, whatever that was, take it or leave it. Like they say, what you see is what you get. No morning after surprises sans makeup.

"We've had a rash of traffickers cruising Lloyd's Center mall for runaways to sell to the Canadians."

The usual. To Fox the business was so revolting he could no longer stand that part of the job at Vice. Too many times he'd been in on a raid at a cheap motel on Sandy Boulevard to rescue some drugged kid who thought she'd swap sex for a chance to get a hot shower and a clean bed only to be raped and drugged. It was part of seasoning, the pimps called it, breaking a girl's spirit so she was compliant.

There was a market in Vancouver, BC for fourteen year old girls. Too often the Portland police were too late.

The crime scene where Long Nguen had been dumped was just at the edge of the access road overlooking the view of the Columbia River. It was marked off with yellow tape.

J.J. got out of her car and joined him. He hadn't seen her since he left Vice months before. She was wearing black slacks and a waterproof thigh length black coat that looked expensive. It was a modest as you could get without wearing a full burka and gloves.

Caryl asked, "Who found the body?"

"Couple of kids walking their dog. The dog made a fuss or the kids wouldn't have seen her down in the bushes."

"Hal told me she was found partially naked. Any articles of clothing left behind?"

J.J. shook her head.

"Hal told me she was choked to death on her panties. No clothing missing?"

"Wouldn't be the first time." Serial killers often saved souvenirs. Caryl remembered worse cases, other souvenirs, like cut off body parts. One Oregon serial killer had kept breasts in the garage deep freezer. Never told his wife. He got life without parole.

There was nothing more to be seen at Rocky Butte. Next stop: the medical examiner.

J.J. knew the way so Caryl followed her down 82nd Street to Clackamas.

As they waited outside the office Caryl explained, "Hal wants us to team up on this. I've been looking for the girl as my only lead in the Hamilton murder." He explained the situation at the Rose Plaza and the ritual murder. He had copied the pictures from Hamilton's cell phone to his own and showed her. "That's the tattoo."

She suggested, "You might trace the art to a local tattoo shop." She gave him an ironic smile. "There are dozens of tattoo parlors nowadays, not counting the artists who work on their own or do the work for friends."

"Expensive."

"Sometimes they barter."

About forty percent of people between eighteen and thirty-five had tattoos. It was a recent cultural phenomenon, no longer limited to sailors and marines on shore leave. It was no longer a stigma. Now respectable people had tattoos. Even Starbucks was permitting their employees to show them. Using your body as a canvas was like a badge of honor, an initiation rite. People were proud of their first tattoo. Every one had a story.

Caryl Fox did not want a tattoo. Police were always asking for distinguishing marks as identification. If he were working under cover, a tattoo might be a dead giveaway as in turning up dead in the trunk of a car sunk in the Willamette River.

They were finally admitted and the girl's body shown on a stainless steel examining table. Long's face had been battered and bruised so she hardly resembled the selfie Fox had shown around the gentlemen's clubs and provided to the Portland Tribune. The tattoo on her shaved pudenda was unmistakable.

"That's her," Caryl said. "It looks like someone waned to make her an example. Was she raped?"

The medical examiner frowned. Medical examiners see any manner of corpses, from skeletal remains to crushed victims of auto accidents "Anal penetration with a foreign object, possibly a broom handle. When we do the autopsy I think we'll find the colon ruptured. It was probably done to inflict maximum pain."

The very thought of it made Caryl's butt cringe. "Nasty."

The look on J.J.'s face suggested she had a similar reaction. "Like this is what happens when you cheat on your pimp. Maybe the thing she had going with your Major Hamilton was an attempt to break away from the business."

"You mean she might want to marry him to get out of the sex trade?"

"That or she was doing tricks on the side and keeping all the money. Pimps don't like that."

Caryl had to agree. His mind turned to another possible paper trail: did the Major pay her in cash? You didn't pay a hooker with a credit card or a check. Checks bounce and lead crooks to your account. With the routing number it was easy to order a book of checks and draw on the account. Hooking was a cash only business, untraceable. "That's one scenario, but it doesn't explain Major Hamilton's murder. Somehow they are tied together."

J.J. sighed. "Maybe her boy friend wanted to punish her and take revenge on the Major. That selfie you showed to the TV folks linked them."

"Wrong time line. The Major was already dead when I released the photo. Normally she'd be beaten up to give out the name of her client, and then it would be his turn."

J.J. agreed. "We'll interview who ever comes in to identify the body and go from there. We have her address. We'll talk to her neighbors and family members. Someone has to know something."

"If they'll talk. The Vietnamese are a pretty tight community." Caryl suggested, "It might help the investigation if you were a Buddhist."

"Let's keep our religious preferences out of this."

Caryl nodded. "No offense intended."

"None taken." J.J. turned to the medical examiner.

The medical examiner was young and looked like he just got out of college. New lab coat without the usual stains.

J.J. gave him her card. "When someone shows up to identify the body, keep them waiting until we can get here to interview them. Get all their ID vitals. Can't have someone show up anonymously and disappear."

"What about the girl's parents?" Caryl asked." Have they been notified?"

"We haven't located them yet. Nguen is a pretty common name among the Vietnamese. Like Smith."

Chapter twelve

Following the information on the dead woman's driver's license, Caryl followed J.J. to Long Nguen's address on Division. It was time to talk to neighbors and the girl's partner if she had one.

It was one of those twelve plexes, typically built on a lot that had once been the site of a big single family residence, torn down and replaced with multi-family, part of Portland's response to the limits of the urban growth boundary. Portland's population was growing by many thousands every year, putting a strain on infrastructure and threatening urban sprawl. The result was more congestion in higher density neighborhoods. Homes built for single families didn't need six or twelve parking spaces on the street, but condos did, much to the ire of the people who were already there.

Not only that, but Victorian homes with character were being replaced by sterile apartments thrown up out of cheap lumber, chip board sealed with Tyvek and covered with siding or, worse, big panels. Such buildings were supposed to have a life of about thirty years and be torn down, not like the original homes built to last a hundred years or more. The mass-produced stock, single pane windows were flush with the outside walls. There was no such thing as a balcony. It was one step up from a barracks, but was supposed to pass for afAudiable housing.

Long Nguen's apartment was on the third floor, no elevator. Four apartments were on each floor, two facing the front, two the rear.

It was convenient that whoever killed Ms. Nguen had left her purse behind, evidence that whoever killed her wanted the world to know who she was and that she was dead.. There had been no money in it of course, but she had a driver's license and a SNAP debit card, the equivalent of what used to be called food stamps. She didn't have a car key, just a single door key which J.J. used to let Caryl and herself into the building.

Caryl Fox didn't like the building because he had seen how they were constructed. There were smoke alarms, if they worked. If there was a fire you had to be quick to get out, for the whole place could be an inferno in five minutes. They climbed the stairs, avoiding a tricycle that had been left in the hall and knocked.

It took a long time before anyone answered. J.J. was about to use Long's key to let them in when someone inside responded.

"Portland Police. We need to talk to you."

The door opened about three inches on the safety chain and a dark eye peered out. "What is it?"

J.J. showed her badge. "We need to talk to you about Long Nguen."

"What about? She been arrested?"

"May we come in, please?"

The chain was unhooked and the door opened. J.J. went in first, Caryl Fox at her heel, showing his badge, too.

The apartment was furnished with what looked like a recycled Goodwill couch. What stood out was a pole in the middle of the room. Caryl's assumption about pole dancing had been correct. It looked like Long had worked out in the apartment.

He let J.J. lead. She introduced them both and asked "Who are you? Lung's roommate?"

"Lotus Nguen. I'm Long's sister."

That put a different cast to their visit. J.J. broke the news. "I'm very sorry to tell you that she has been murdered."

Oddly Lotus Nguen was not surprised. If she grieved, she didn't show it. You would expect her to be shocked, maybe get hysterical with grief. She didn't. Her only show of emotion was she bit her lip, no tears. "I warned her. Her business… she called it being an escort…is dangerous."

J.J suggested, "Escort is a polite name for it."

"She has regular clients."

"Did she ever mention Major Hamilton?" Caryl showed the selfie photo.

"She see him every Friday. Her boy friend not like that."

"Boy friend?"

"His name is Tyrone. Tyrone Brown."

J.J. knew him. "He's a pimp. They always pretend to be boy friends."

From his work in Vice Caryl knew that as part of the seasoning process pimps wooed girls into believing that they loved them, that is, the smooth ones. Others simply raped and drugged the girls unto submission. Maybe Tyrone had not got as far as turning Long into his sex slave. The girls were seldom able to quit.

Lotus insisted, "My sister is not a prostitute."

So, Long had used her sister's name for her business pseudonym. Though Caryl Fox had never seen her except in photos and on the examiner's steel table, he thought the sister was taller.

"Are you both pole dancers?"

"No. She is. I practice sometimes. I work in a restaurant."

"When did you see her last?"

"She didn't come home last night. She was here early but she said she was to meet a client."

Client? That was a nice name for a john. "What sort of client?"

Lotus shrugged her shoulders evasively. "A man. She have appointment."

J.J. feigned naiveté., "What sort of appointment?"

"She said escort. I think for sex."

So Long wasn't one of the typical 82nd street hookers. "What about her relationship with Major Hamilton?"

"I think she want to marry him." Her expression showed that she thought it was a stupid idea. "He old man much too old."

J.J. agreed. "Maybe he was the one who thought about getting married."

Caryl shook his head. "Why buy the cow if you get the milk for free?"

J.J. laughed. "I'm sure it wasn't free."

"Yeh, right." Caryl took out his cell phone and flipped through the evidence photos. He showed Lotus the one of the thong underwear. "Do you recognize this?"

She knew it. "She wear one like that. Just for business. Not comfortable."

Caryl agreed. He had tried a thong before his change. They weren't sanitary. Now he wore jockey shorts.

J.J. was apologetic. "We're sorry to have brought you such bad news. We need to contact your parents. How can we find them?"

"They live in Texas. Austin. I can give you address." She looked for an address book in a drawer of the telephone table. It was furniture left over from the days when everyone had a land line. Now most people had cell phones. She turned to the page and tried to dictate the address, fumbled on the pronunciation of the Spanish street name. Finally, exasperated, she handed the book to J.J. who copied down the information as well as she could.

If would be up to the Austin police to break the news in person. Phone calls to people who might be alone and not able to take the shock were not a good way to communicate. A death was difficult enough to report. Murder was worse.

Knowing the parents were in Texas and not in Portland told Caryl that this was not likely to be a family honor killing. At least that was one factor he could cross off his list of potentials. If you are suspicious enough, anybody could be the perp. Weird things happened in weird Portland.

She handed the book to Caryl for corroboration. The script was foreign, but the phone numbers were easy enough.

J.J suggested they knock on a few doors and see if anyone had seen Long picked up. They needed a lead on the so-called client. If Major Hamilton was her Friday night regular, who did she see on other nights? Maybe she had more than one "old man" client on her string. Someone beside Tyrone Brown might be possessive and jealous.

Chapter thirteen

Caryl accompanied J.J. as they knocked on doors of the twelve-plex, but at that time of day hardly anyone was home. One of the apartments was the home of a Ukrainian family, but the wife, who was cradling a crying baby, spoke no English and neither J.J. nor Caryl spoke Ukrainian or Russian.

J.J. and Caryl parted company in the parking lot. Caryl wanted to get back to the Rose Plaza. He needed something that linked Long to Major Hamilton's murder. Did she visit him frequently, or was that a one time deal? Was the relationship just professional, or did she have long term ideas? Maybe nobody knew.

Caryl also wanted to interview the Plaza security guard. Had Long had been signed in as a visitor or sneaked in after hours? Did she use her real name, or just Lotus? An old man bringing in an Asian hooker at night would have attracted attention at the Rose Plaza. Maybe not at some motels, but certainly at the Rose Plaza retirement home.

Maybe she could have come in pretending to deliver a pizza or Chinese takeout with a side order of sex.

The parking lot at the Rose Plaza was full and the valet service in place. Detective Fox wasn't about to hand over the keys to the police car to some kid and was directed to a service spot reserved for visiting doctors at the Metcalf Assisted Living wing.

It gave him a chance to check out the back entrance.

He used Hamilton's fob to get in the back door. He noted the interior CCT camera mounted in the ceiling above the back entrance, but it did not have an unobstructed view of the freight elevator. The back entrance was in full view of the nurse's station, but was it staffed all the time?

Because the Rose Plaza was built on a slope, the west parking lot at the back entered on the second floor. He took the freight elevator down to the ground floor from there and discovered the garden entrance on the east side.

One could get in there, also with a fob. There was a CCT camera there, too.

Glad his rain jacket had a hood, he walked in the rain around the garden path to the breezeway and the main entrance. The visitors' sign-in sheets at the welcome desk were barely legible but went back for about a week. No signature resembled anything like Lotus or Long. No one had visited Hamilton's twelfth floor apartment. Lotus had not signed in, but she had been there. He had proof of that.

He still didn't believe that a pretty Asian girl was capable of cutting out a man's liver while he watched. You couldn't judge by appearances. Dictator Assad in Syria looked like a mild mannered dentist, not a war criminal. George Bundy had been a good looking guy, too. Neither had any qualms about murder.

"What are you looking for, Detective?" It was that snoopy Mrs. Seller, this time wearing a red beret and being curious, and hanging out by the front desk..

"I'm trying to figure out how Major Hamilton's girl friend got into the building. I've checked the CCT records and the sign in sheet."

She smirked. "I can show you how."

"Really?"

"The Mystery Club is always thinking about crimes."

"The Mystery Club?"

"We have a group of residents who read crime novels written by women. You know women are the best creators of crime novels."

Hadn't she told him that before? Maybe she was at the age when you epeated yourself, forgetting what went before. "I don't read crime novels. I have enough crime in my job." Files of case studies with the on scene photographs were more than enough for him.

She could relate to that. "Confidentially, we've had several murders here in the Rose Plaza. Even one of our Mystery Club members. Poisoned. I'm practically the last survivor."

"Sounds like a club not to be a member of."

"I don't mean the members have all been murdered. They just died. Goes with the territory."

"The territory?" He didn't get it.

"The average age here is 86, detective. Someone dies every month."

He had avoided thinking about his own death. Death was what happened to other people. Preferably very old people. Philosophically one could conclude that life was a fatal condition ending at the grave.

She interrupted his momentary distraction. "Death is the price we pay for life, Mr. Fox, or is it Ms?"

Caryl resented the dig. "Just call me detective. Caryl will also do."

"Well Caryl, follow me and I'll show you how someone can get into the building undetected."

Curious, Fox dutifully followed Mrs. Seller. First to the private dining room. There was actually an emergency exit at the back.

"That leads to the parking lot," she explained, but if someone came in that way, here's too much activity in the lobby. That's not how I'd get in. Let's go up to the twelfth floor."

They returned to the lobby and the main elevators.

At the twelfth floor she led Detective Fox down the long hallway to the end where Major Hamilton's apartment was out of sight of the CCT camera watching over the pair of main elevators.

The door to the apartment that was being remodeled was open. The two Mexican sheet rock workers were gone, replaced by a couple of painters, also foreign. A sheet of paper was taped in the doorway to keep from tracking dirt into the hallway.

Fox knocked, didn't want to leave any footprints. "Hello?"

One of the painters came over. He was wearing white painter's trousers, splotched with so many colors his outfit could have been mounted at the Portland Art Museum as a modern installation. He was dark skinned, though not African American.

Fox showed his badge. "I'm Detective Fox investigating the murder of the Major across the hall. Were you working here last weekend?"

Head shake. "No."

"The remodel crew seems to be international. Where are you from? "

"I'm from Philippines. My partner is Cuban."

"Your name?"

"Elan. My partner is Jesus."

Fox knew that male Moslems were usually named Mohammed after the prophet. Jesus was a common name, but he always found it odd for someone to have the name of God."

Mrs. Seller was impatient. "You want to see how to get in the building."

"Yes."

She pointed to an overhead exit sign. "This is the south stairway. Nobody uses it, but it leads to the parking lot. I could walk you down, but my knees don't do twelve flights of stairs. We'll take the freight elevator down to the third floor and catch it from there."

"Not the second floor?"

"The second floor is the nurses' station and the assisted living section. It's on the parking lot level."

On the third floor there it was, the last flight of the south fire escape stairway. "I can do this much," Mrs. Seller said. Carefully holding the hand rail, she took the stairs one step at a time down to the bottom. A prominent sign there said, "For security reasons, do not prop open this door."

"You can't enter from the outside," Mrs. Seller explained, "but someone inside could let someone in. Or you could tape the lock like the Watergate burglars did."

They stepped out into the parking lot and the rain. Mrs. Seller quickly let herself in the back entrance, leaving Caryl Fox to get a good look around. Sure enough, there was no fob entrance to this door and no CCT camera. Someone inside might see the door through the nurses' station window, but how much traffic might there be at night when those elderly patients would be in their beds?

This was a possibility. It didn't mean that it was actually the way Lotus was let into the building, but it could be done. The Major had been a recluse, wanted his privacy. He might not want people to know he was smuggling a hooker into the Rose Plaza after hours. He might be paranoid about being observed.

Caryl Fox was getting to know more about Major Hamilton. Why take a whore to a motel where you had to sign in and pay when you had a swell apartment on the twelfth floor? As in Shakespeare's plays, everyone has a fatal character flaw. Caryl would admit that his own ambiguity about sexual preference might be his. What was Hamilton's?

The man had been a bundle of contradictions. The kill book showed a killer, but he also had a thing for Asian women. What else would his history reveal?

Chapter thirteen

He needed to follow up on Mrs. Grafton's tip about the veterans group. He had written the name Bill Cooper in his notebook and had the Plaza directory. To his surprise he discovered that Cooper had an eleventh floor apartment directly below Hamilton's.

Luckily Cooper was in. He was dressed in a pair of slacks with cargo pockets and a tee shirt with a frayed collar. If Fox had ever imagined an old face, this would have been it. Like many old people. Cooper had lost the subcutaneous fat under the skin, so it was nearly transparent, showing blue veins. He was nearly bald, the skin an uneven color over a bumpy skull like it had been reconstructed by a neophyte brain surgeon.

Caryl showed his badge. "I'm detective Fox of homicide. Your upstairs neighbor, Major Hamilton was murdered some time over the weekend.. Did you hear any strange noises since, say, last Friday night?"

As if to answer his question there was a grinding noise that would drive a hearing person out. The remodel crew upstairs was it.

Cooper pointed to his left ear. "If it gets too loud I just take out my hearing aids."

"I see."

"I got them from the VA. Got thirty percent disability."

His wasn't telling Fox anything about Hamilton. "Did you serve with Major Hamilton?" It was a long shot.

"Oh, no. He's Vietnam era. I flew in World War II."

My God, Fox thought. This is a genuine member of the greatest generation. Fox knew almost nothing about

World War II except it ended in 1945 before he was born. "You must be about ninety."

"Ninety-two. Flew B17s over Germany. Did you hear about the American who was landing at Templehof and didn't know where to park his plane?"

Fox didn't know what Templehof was, presumably an air field.

"So German air controller asks, "Haven't you been here before?"

Fox waited for the punch line.

"He says, 'I did, but I didn't land.'"

Fox didn't get it until Cooper proudly added, "I bombed Templehof on the first raid over Berlin."

"Oh."

Cooper was clearly disappointed not to have an appreciative audience. "What did you want, Detective?"

"What do you know about Major Hamilton?"

"Not much. We asked him to speak at one of our monthly lunches. At first he was eager, mentioned Laos and the Ho Chi Min trail, but when it got down to it he backed out."

"Why was that?"

"He said it was all classified. I think he had PTSD. Talk about the war set him off. Whatever he did, he didn't want to talk about it. He wouldn't even come to any of the lunches after that."

"Any idea why?"

Cooper shook his head. "Maybe talking about his service would bring back nightmares. I used to have them myself. On my twelfth mission I got shot down. Landed in France. The underground got me to the Spanish border. Then back to England, but they didn't let you fly after that in case you got shot down again and were captured. The Germans wanted to know how flyers were helped to escape."

Fox could see that Cooper had a lot of stories to tell, but what he wanted was anything about Major Hamilton. "If you can tell me anything about the major, give me a call." He handed over one of his business cards.

The racket from the floor above began again.

Cooper looked at the card and gave him a disappointed look. "I was hoping you were from the noise abatement committee. I complained."

Didn't Cooper remember that Caryl showed his badge? He must be stuck in his old war stories. Fox shrugged. "I guess you just have to take out your hearing aids."

On reflection he realized that for combat veterans the most exciting moment in their lives was military service. Those memories stuck. All that came after was just a post script.

Cooper enjoyed talking about his wartime adventures. Hamilton would not. Was he hiding something? Was it so horrible he couldn't face it? Or was he ashamed?

As he made his way back to the main elevators he wondered why Hamilton wouldn't talk to the veterans lunch. He had shown his son pictures from Vietnam. Maybe that's why his son called him a war criminal.

The Vietnam war was a long time ago. He had no experience or memory of it. They didn't mention it in school.

When Caryl Fox had been a kid he preferred jeans to silly dresses. Toy trucks appealed more to him than plastic soldiers. He'd been too young to think about war. His father didn't like guns and wouldn't allow war games. How different that was from the combat veterans. Their experiences stayed with them, like forever.

Fox had not actually served in any war, not in Iraq I or Iraq II. . He had only been in the military long enough to get thrown out because of his sexual preference. At least the discharge was under honorable circumstances. It wasn't dishonorable to want a sex change. It wasn't an undesirable discharge, either. Or a general discharge without benefits. He'd got a military lawyer to persuade the army to call it a release for medical reasons. That had been his only win in a losing situation.

He'd better contact the Major's son again. Something in that military history might be relevant. He had the kill book at the office. He'd study that some more.

Chapter fourteen

It was only under duress that Major Hamilton's son Arthur flew out to Portland. He had to see that lawyer at Frizbee and Cachum for the reading of the will. At least he had the courtesy to phone Detective Fox first in case the will might include a clue to who might have murdered the Major.

Always suspicious of people's motives, Caryl thought it wasn't only a courtesy. Arthur Hamilton probably wanted a witness to show that he had no idea what was in the will or what his father's estate consisted of. He knew only that Major Hamilton had wanted to be buried in the National Cemetery in Portland where he would have an honor guard, a three gun salute, and a flag.

In order to have an opportunity for a private, one on one conversation with Arthur Hamilton, Caryl offered to pick him up at PDX. With a marking pen he made a cardboard sign that said "Hamilton" and waited.

Waited was the operative word, for the plane was delayed. Eventually a middle-aged man about forty and wearing a heavy jacket, no hat, separated from the crowd of travelers coming off the gate. Weather was bad in Syracuse, Arthur explained, and he missed a connection for a direct flight to Portland. He ended up changing planes in Chicago at O'Hare, an airport he hated. At least, flying east to west, he gained three hours flying from Eastern to Pacific time.

Arthur Hamilton hardly resembled his father. He was of mixed race, one of what some called the rainbow people. Noticing that immediately, Caryl assumed that Arthur was adopted. He had seen a framed wedding photo of the Major and his white bride. Was Arthur a Vietnamese orphan? Or the result of an affair between the Major and a Vietnamese girl? It was not uncommon for Koreans, Japanese and Vietnamese women to couple with American GIs. The trouble was, in those countries, especially Korea, a child of mixed race was a non person. It was the Asian equivalent of what the Nazis called Rassenschande, a pollution of the Aryan race. In the United States they used to call it miscegenation. There was more than one definition of what it meant to be Aryan, racially pure. Pearl Buck had written a book about it. What did it mean for Arthur Hamilton to be of mixed race?

Caryl didn't dare ask. Really, it was none of his business, but if it shed light on the Major, it might help solve his murder. Maybe after a few beers he might have the opportunity to ask Arthur Hamilton about his origins. That might explain the Major's fixation on Asian girls.

Caryl reasoned that a GI would not have been able to marry a Vietnamese girl, certainly not in those hectic days at the end of a war. Did the Major rescue the baby from the North Vietnamese Communists, whom he hated, or was the baby his own kid?

Society was full of mixtures. Portland was tolerant, international and multicultural, but not everyone in the world was. Caryl was transgender and his erstwhile partner J.J., who was a Moslem convert in a culture riddled with Islamophobia, were not accepted in the Portland policed force as "one of us."

How did Arthur Hamilton fit into the mix in Syracuse? Caryl had never been to New York State. Was Syracuse as lily white as Salem, Oregon?

One advantage of driving a patrol car was Caryl could just park it on the street at the terminal. He opened the back door so Hamilton could stow his carry-on in the back seat. "Sit in front so people won't think you are a prisoner."

The front seat was crowded with radio, GPS, and a computer screen, but Hamilton squeezed in and buckled up. As they pulled away onto the access road he asked, "You didn't say on the phone how my father was killed."

Caryl was cautious. "You can see for yourself. I'll take you right to the medical examiner's office to identify him. You'll need to do that anyway. One of those official identification procedures."

"That still doesn't tell me anything. What was he, shot?"

"Ultimately he had his throat cut. It was a sort of ritual murder."

Hamilton was still trying to digest the information. "How do you mean?"

"His liver was cut out. A piece of it, anyway." Caryl took his eyes off the traffic long enough to get a look art Hamilton's face. He had gone pale. "You aren't going to be sick on me, are you?"

"My dad told me about that stuff. Sometimes the South Vietnamese troops would tie a Viet Kong to a tree and eat his liver while he stood there, watching."

Caryl had only given the kill book a quick glance. The photos were repugnant. "I have his photo album at the precinct. We could go over it."

Hamilton sighed. "You know about My Lai?"

"What was that?" To Caryl the past history of the Vietnam war was just as mysterious and distant as Bill Cooper's bombing of Berlin in World War II.

"It was an atrocity, a war crime. But it was not the only one. There were several, though not as well known as My Lai. My dad was in one of those. You know, the GIs see their buddies killed and go berserk, kill everyone in a village, including babies."

Caryl didn't know about Vietnam, but he had followed the more recent story of the American who, drunk, went into an Afghan village and murdered sixteen people, including mothers and children. He got an eight year prison sentence in an American court. With luck he could be out on parole in five or six. "So you accused your father of being a war criminal."

"Right."

"Never charged?"

"No."

"You never forgave him?"

That evoked an outburst from Arthur Hamilton. "What? Not me. If anyone was to forgive him, it had to be some Vietnamese."

"Did you know he had an Asian girl friend in Portland, a prostitute? I've got her picture. Will show it to you later."

Arthur Hamilton didn't want to see it. "My father was one twisted guy."

This was Caryl's opportunity. "Was your birth mother Vietnamese?"

"Yes, my mother was Vietnamese but I never met her."

"Do you know if your dad was your birth father?"

"He kept that part of his past a secret. It was a taboo subject in our household. My mother couldn't have kids of her own. She never accepted me. It was not a happy childhood."

Caryl was puzzled. "You told me your dad hated communists, but then he has a half Vietnamese son."

"Not all Vietnamese were communists."

Now Caryl's ignorance was showing. "Of course not. Like they say in church, hate the sin but not the sinner."

That didn't go down well with Arthur Hamilton. "I don't know what you're talking about. Being a communist isn't a sin."

Caryl could see talking with Arthur Hamilton risked major misunderstanding and even hostility. He changed the subject. "We checked his computer. He had a thing for young Asian girls."

"My Dad was a complicated guy. He hated the war, but when he was in it he was a killer. I think the contradiction was a mental thing. I know he had PTSD. Most combat vets do, to one degree or another. Only the die hard psychopaths love to kill."

"I'm told he was a recluse. Maybe that was part of his PTSD." Caryl felt out of his depth on that subject. If

Hamilton's PTSD was part of his medical record, it might be helpful to check at the VA hospital.

How would knowing about Hamilton's PTSD solve his murder? The war was a long time ago and had nothing to do with life in the Rose Plaza and any enemies he might have made in Portland.

There was possible a connection with Long Nguen's murder. Her sister said she had a boy friend, Tyrone something or other. Might be jealousy. Was she actually married? He didn't know that. It wasn't so unusual that a husband pimped for his own wife, but what if she took a shine to her clients? .

Arthur was thoughtful. "I don't know what he was going the last couple of years. If he went to some VA support group where they talk about their nightmares, he might have talked about the massacre. If he did, someone might have blabbed."

Caryl didn't know how those support groups worked. He did know that PTSD was a major cause of homelessness among Portland's veterans. Combat was so stressful and terrifying the nightmares and flashbacks could mentally cripple someone. Some vets were afraid of crowds. Maybe that was why Hamilton stayed in his apartment at the Plaza. Or maybe there was some other reason.

Chapter fifteen

The rain had diminished to a soak. The Willamette river would be rising. Caryl hated freeway driving in the rain. Trucks threw up blinding clouds of spray.

They arrived at the Clackamas medical examiner's office Even the waiting room at the office smelled of formalin and death.

The attendant doctor met them with a wry smile. "So, Detective Fox, back again? Can't stay away from corpses?"

"I've brought Major Hamilton's son to identify his father." He turned to Arthur. "You sure you're ready for this?"

Arthur Hamilton was stoic. He'd mentally prepared for this. "Got to do it. I haven't seen him in years. I hope I recognize him."

The examiner rolled out the body of Major Hamilton and pulled back the sheet. "That him?"

With the passage of rigor mortis the facial expression that at first had registered terror and pain had relaxed.

Arthur Hamilton swallowed and nodded. "That's him." He bent for a close look. "I see how his throat was cut. Will you show the rest, please?"

The sheet was pulled back showing the chest and the gap where part of the liver had been cut out. The blood had been cleaned up.

"Here we go again."

Caryl was puzzled. "What do you mean by that?"

"What goes around comes around."

It wasn't clear to Caryl. "Meaning?"

"Put it another way, detective. The golden rule: don't do to others what you wouldn't have done to you."

"You think Major Hamilton cut people's livers in Vietnam?"

Arthur shook his head. "I don't know. Some GI's collected ears of their kills, like Indians used to collect scalps. So far as I know all my dad took was pictures. I don't think he collected livers."

Caryl Fox collected nothing, had no mementos except that one strapless party dress. He remembered Mrs. Seller's comment about Mrs. Hamilton collecting matchbooks. At least it wasn't ears or scalps.

The medical examiner had covered up the Major's body and was putting it back in storage. "Want to see his girl friend? The one in the selfie?"

"Girl friend?"

"I didn't tell you," Caryl explained. "We found a selfie on your father's cell phone. Showed him with an Asian girl we have since identified. We posted the photo in the hopes that someone would identify her. I think someone who saw it didn't like the association with your father."

For a moment Caryl had a pang of guilt. Posting the photo may have brought on her death. He dismissed the unhappy thought. "She was murdered. Body's here. Want to see it?"

"Why not? As long as I'm here."

She was produced.

Arthur looked down at her face. "Dad had a thing for Vietnamese women. Too bad."

"Choked to death on her own underwear," the examiner explained. He leered. "Want to see her tattoo?" What was this? Some prurient interest on the part of the medical examiner?

Caryl had the photo from the Major's cell phone. "Let's pass on that one. Even a corpse deserves some modesty."

For someone accustomed to all the gory details, the medical examiner had long since lost any inhibitions about seeing private parts. "Suit yourself."

Before they could go further, Caryl's cell phone rang. It was J.J. "I've got the name and address of Long's pimp. Why don't you meet me at her place and we can scout him out together? I need backup for this one."

"I'll just drop Arthur Hamilton at the Rose Plaza and be right with you. Might take half an hour."

Caryl drove Arthur Hamilton back over the Willamette river on the new Sellwood bridge and north on Macadam, the shortest route back to the Rose Plaza. He pulled up at the breezeway and handed Hamilton the major's keys. "You have to sign in at the front desk. The fob is necessary to get in the entrance doors. The black key is to his car in the garage. Oh, and here's my card with my phone number at the precinct. I have the photo album there and want to go over it with you. Right now I have a pimp to catch."

Chapter sixteen

Driving a squad car to the airport was convenient, but parking a squad car on the street outside Long's apartment building attracted attention and suspicion. People watched the street. The neighborhood wasn't safe.

After hooking up with J.J. Caryl decided to park the squad car in a lot by a Burger King and accompany JJ in her unmarked. Lotus Nguen was not eager to give out any information, especially not the name of her sister's boy friend. She said he was dangerous. He wouldn't want her to finger him to the police. J.J. cautioned that withholding information was an offense, so she was finally persuaded. The name of her sister's boy friend was Tyrone Brown.

A quick computer check pulled up Brown's record. As a juvenile he'd been arrested for stealing cars, released on probation, arrested again and released again. It was a revolving door for car thieves the police didn't want to clog the jails with. Joyriding was one thing. If Tyrone Brown had been feeding luxury cars to the export trade, that might have been different. Owning a luxury car in a seaport like Portland, Oregon risked it being put in a container for resale in the Far East or an Arab country.

Brown had graduated to a couple of assault charges, basically bar fights but he had never used a firearm or even a knife. Disorderly conduct and aggravated assault. Got a one year sentence, suspended. Probation. Possession of meth got him a year but released early during general amnesty to reduce the pressure on overcrowded jails.

Then he got into the sex trade. Being a pimp was less conspicuous. If you ran half a dozen girls you could make big money. As long as the women got enough drugs and were afraid to go to the police, they were the ones who took the risks.

Brown's booking photo showed a scowling black face, dreadlocks, and a nascent mustache. J.J. and Caryl had no trouble finding Brown's address. He had a basement apartment in a building with several exits so he could slip away fast. Being in a basement meant neighbors couldn't hear unusual noises, like screams.

Brown wasn't there. Nobody in the building who was home knew him as anything but a quiet guy who dressed in black leather and didn't make any trouble. One neighbor kid who should have been in school said Brown drove an old black Camero that needed paint, not a gaudy pimpmobile with tasseled windows and dice dangling from the rear view mirror. It was a car that, parked on a dark street, would be virtually invisible. The car hadn't been seen lately.

So who did Long have an "appointment" with? If not Tyrone, then who? Some john? Hooking was a dangerous profession. Some serial killers felt they were doing a moral duty to clean up the streets by murdering prostitutes. Who else would be stupid enough to get into a car with a stranger late at night?

J.J. took the initiative and used the police car's computer to search the vehicle registration database for the license plate for Brown's Camero. Portland had several cars equipped with license plate readers. While the car cruised the city it noted every vehicle and could track the location and activities of specific cas. Some people were aware of the program and protested, but it was important for following drug dealers, etc. Where was Brown's car?

Tyrone Brown's Camero had been spotted in the parking lot at Lloyd's Center and outside the Pink Bunny motel on Barbur Boulevard, one of those motels where you could rent a room by the hour. That was two days ago. It was the best surveillance they could do more or less automatically without tracking Brown's cell phone or planting a GPS locator in the car itself. As a small time hoodlum he was not important enough to lay on a full court press. Portland didn't have the resources. So where was he? Where had he been when Long was strangled?

J.J. drove Caryl to the Burger King to pick up the squad car.

On the way he told her about Arthur Hamilton. Caryl suspected that Arthur was not an orphan picked up at random when Americans were hastily pulling out of Saigon, but actually his own son by a Vietnamese woman who had stayed behind. He reasoned that if Mrs. Hamilton could not have children and resented her husband adopting a bastard baby from Vietnam that would not make for a happy marriage. No wonder the mixed race son said he had an unhappy childhood.

Major Hamilton had a safety deposit box at the Umpqua Bank branch at the Rose Plaza where documents like a birth certificate or certificate of adoption might be kept. With the Major dead, the box would be sealed until the executor was present for the opening.

That meant an appointment with that lawyer Frizbee. They would all have to meet at the bank and take an inventory of what was in the Major's box.

Arthur Hamilton did not know the identity of his birth mother. Perhaps she was still alive, but where? Would this have any bearing on the Major's murder? Caryl had the safety deposit key found in the Major's computer desk drawer. He would have to arrange for the lawyer Frizbee and Arthur Hamilton to be present when they opened the box.

In the meantime he drove back to the first precinct to mull over that photo album. There might be something in it that he had missed. If Tyrone Brown had a cell phone, they could locate him. Pimps were J.J.'s department in Vice. Caryl hated slime bags like Tyrone Brown that preyed on runaway girls and even boys. That was one of the reasons he transferred out of Vice. To Caryl's mind, Brown was a prime suspect in the girl's murder, but was there any connection to the murder of

Major Hamilton? Too bad Long's phone was blocked, for it was sure to have her pimp's number in it.

Chapter seventeen

They got lucky. While he sat in Detective Casey's old office in the first precinct, with its old filing cabinets and the ghosts of unsolved cases, J.J. called him to say Tyrone Brown had been stopped at the Canadian border trying to smuggle a drugged, white fourteen year old girl into Canada. At first he tried to claim that he was the kid's father and had permission to cross the border, then said she was just a hitchhiker he had given a lift. Neither story stuck. She didn't have an ID.

It took immigration only minutes to find Brown on their computer. It turned out he was on probation. To leave the country was a violation and he'd be sent back. Someone would have to come and pick him up. J.J. had her own idea." He was probably planning to sell the girl in Vancouver BC."

I was a typical pattern in the sex trafficking business. The I-5 corridor didn't just facilitate movement of semi trucks up and down the coast. It also transported drugs from Mexico and sex slaves to Canada.

Caryl commented to J.J. "Did he expect a black guy with a white girl could cross the border without her ID and parent's permission? How could he be so dumb?"

J.J. snickered. "Most criminals are about as smart as a trout. He must be new at this aspect of the business."

Caryl wasn't a fisherman but he'd heard trout were pretty smart. "When did he get picked up?"

"Yesterday."

"Shit. Then he has a perfect alibi. He couldn't have strangled Long Nguen."

"Don't be so sure. Brown's been in jail. He could have made a contact with someone who owes him a favor, like killing his whore."

It was true that in exchange for protection while in prison parolees were beholden to the gangs inside. "Who's going to bring Brown back to Portland?"

"Maybe a US Marshall. They're not going to put him in a taxi."

"Was he arrested on the Canadian side?"

"Lucky for us, no, but it was in Washington and there's that whole extradition thing if he wants to fight it. He might be persuaded to waive extradition if it's just as trafficking charge. If he knows he's identified as a person of interest in Long's murder, he might fight it."

"That doesn't help me in the murder of Major Hamilton."

J.J. agreed. "There may be no connection. Just a coincidence."

Caryl sighed. She was right. Just because you have an Asian girl friend doesn't mean you're a candidate for a ritual murder. It was true that some ethnic groups were particularly angry if a girl dated or married outside the clan. Even Portland had had an honor killing when a Moslem girl married outside her religion. In an honor killing it was always the girl who was the victim, not her boy friend. Jews might consider a child dead for marrying outside the faith, but they didn't kill them.

Caryl was stuck. He was relatively new to this job. So far the cases he had were pretty simple. Domestic violence. Suicide by cop saved law enforcement the trouble and expense of arresting, charging, going to court and convicting. A confession admitting guilt saved the system a protracted court case. A drive by shooting, however, might go unsolved. You didn't have to be much of a detective in most cases. But Caryl knew that thirty percent of suspicious deaths were never solved. Maybe some of those killers were a lot smarter than a trout.

The murder of Major Hamilton wasn't a random drive by shooting. It was planned. Hamilton lived in a high security building and seldom went out except, Caryl suspected, to an occasional gentleman's club. His hooker came to him. Caryl didn't know where Hamilton had first made the connection, but Long's roommate said he was a regular client.

He had dismissed the idea of Hamilton being murdered by one of the elderly residences, most of whom were women. Nobody seemed to know Hamilton. Even that snoopy Mrs. Seller had scant information. But there was a staff of a hundred and eighty some people working there, most of them health care workers. There was the maintenance staff, the kitchen, and so on. And it was full of foreigners. Service jobs were the first level of employment for new immigrants, so the Plaza had Cubans, Mexicans, Africans, Philippines, and Russians for starters. That gave him nearly two hundred potential suspects.

Who would want to kill Major Hamilton? It wasn't a robbery. For a fleeting moment he imagined an elderly vampire feasting on the Major's liver while he bled to death. That was too bizarre, even for Portland. The Grimm TV series was filmed there, but that was fantasy entertainment. The Rose Plaza was not a setting for that kind of story.

He called J.J. back. "Long saw Hamilton on Fridays. What about Thursdays? Someone else? If Major Hamilton was a regular customer, maybe Long had others on her client list." Every girl kept a calendar record of her periods. He did, too, until the hormone shots shut down his female periods. It was part of his chemical conversion. "She may have kept an appointment book. Get the names and dates, phone numbers, addresses. "

"I'll ask her. If one of her other so-called clients found out she was servicing the Major, that might be a reason to kill him out of jealousy."

"And strangle her for cheating."

The case was wide open. If was like dropping the proverbial pebble in the pond. The circle of potential suspects kept getting bigger.

Caryl hoped that it would be simple, that the Major was a one off and Long had long range plans, even marriage. The on line marriage sites made a business of hooking up American losers with much younger, compliant Asian wives who married for the green card ticket to America. What about Long? So far as he knew Long was born in the USA. She wouldn't need a green card. Were her parents among those immigrants that poured into the country after the Vietnam War?

She might have had a call from someone who got her number, a word of mouth connection to a previous client. Could be anyone. For all he knew, her number was scrawled on the walls of public toilets. That would be a hopeless thread to pursue. Caryl was almost ready to move Long's murder to Casey's old file of unsolved murders.

He needed to know about her family and friends. A high percentage of murders were committed by people the victim knew. Domestic killings were common. Usually someone got drunk. There was an argument, and the victim was either shot or stabbed multiple times in a fit of rage. If the cops came and the killer wouldn't put down the weapon, bang. End of case.

This wasn't one of those.

So far as Caryl could find out, the reclusive Major didn't actually know anybody but his whore. Was he lonely, or hiding? PTSD could do that to you. Who the hell cared enough about Major Hamilton to kill him?

Not his son.

Caryl stared at the white board where he had posted the photos of the body taken at the crime scene and in the medical examiner's office. It looked to him like a ritual murder. He had never heard of any other similar case, not in Portland or anywhere else in the United States. There were weird cases of cannibalism, like Geofry Downer, that man in Milwaukee, Wisconsin who ate his boy victims and was eventually killed in prison. That the Major was still alive when his liver was cut out was torture and smacked of revenge. What had the Major done that sparked vengefulness?

Caryl had the feeling that there was a Vietnamese connection somehow. Long was a Vietnamese American, born in the USA. But using a Vietnamese prostitute was no big deal. Caryl knew from the Major's hard drive files that he had a thing for Asian girls. Long Nguen was dead, but murdering prostitutes was not unusual. Any woman who took to the streets as a profession risked her life. There didn't have to be any connection between the Major's murder and Long's. That could be a coincidence.

Yet, it was after the selfie was publicized that Long was killed. Caryl suspected that she was punished for her relationship with Hamilton. If it wasn't Tyrone Brown who did it, or ordered the hit, who else? Her father? He needed to know more about her family in case this turned out to be an honor killing.

It had to be something more than the Major's fascination for young Asian girls. Besides Long Nguen, were there any others? And if so, were they in danger, too?

He decided to go through that old photo album to see if there were any clues in it. He had it in a heavy manila envelope and took it out, but found himself staring at it blankly. He felt he wasn't getting any place on this case. His only lead was dead. Tyrone Brown, in custody at the border, had an alibi. Now what?

To make things worse, he wasn't feeling well. Changing your gender wasn't just a matter of attitude and identification. It involved hormones and medication that messed you up. He no longer menstruated. It was like a forced menopause, intense PMS. He had not had a hysterectomy, but the sex change had required massive doses of testosterone. For men who were low in the male hormone, high doses could lead to testicular cancer or heart attacks. Caryl didn't have testicles, but he could have a heart attack, another of those side effects. He was sick.

Being transgender was a lonely state of being, not just because of the sex change, but because of the social interaction or lack of it. Even tolerant so-called normal people didn't always hide their attitude that he was a freak. He wasn't one of those rare hermaphrodites who had organs of both sexes and years ago might have been in a circus side show. Everyone had some personality characteristics of both genders. So some people were gay. Some were AC/DC. He had always wanted to be a man.

Thanks in part to the VA he had some medical support, but the VA psychologists were more occupied with veterans who suffered from PTSD. The combat vets had support groups. There was a high incidence of suicide. When Caryl phoned the VA hospital he always got the message, "If you think of harming yourself, call..." That was OK for the PTSD patients, but there was nobody Caryl could talk to.

He was depressed but he did not think of harming himself. Sometimes he regretted not being like everyone else, comfortable in their gender, living normal lives with normal sex lives, that is, if there was something you could normal that wasn't perfunctory and ultimately boring. Caryl had no sex life. No partner. No friends.

He had a good working relationship with J.J. but she had her own issues, being a Moslem in a society that viewed all of her faith with suspicion. He had once suggested that they do lunch together, but she ate only halal food. She did not do alcohol, either. The only time she would set foot in a bar was when she was on a case. Even an Orthodox Jew might have been game for a drink or a meal of Chinese food at his favorite restaurant..

Caryl also avoided bars. Portland had begun to resemble the wild west. There were too many shootings in bars, arguments that spilled out onto the sidewalk or the parking lot.

All he had now was the job, and he didn't feel like he was doing it very well. He didn't feel like a drudge, but he didn't need any asinine comments about his choice of gender, either.

Resigned, he opened Major Hamilton's photo album in search of clues.

Chapter eighteen

The major's Vietnam era photo album, what Arthur Hamilton called his father's kill book, had the usual pictures of guys in uniform. At that time Hamilton was a lieutenant. When in boot camp Caryl's training sergeant had said that in Vietnam there was a high casualty rate among lieutenants. They came fresh out of officer's school, thought they knew it all, even regarded the troops as expendable resources, not people.

In Vietnam some arrogant new lieutenants died of so-called friendly fire--shot in the back--or were fragged by their own drugged up, angry troops. Caryl didn't think Hamilton had been one of those arrogant wise ass newbies. He had been a hero, after all, got that silver star for saving a wounded buddy.

What had the citation read? Hamilton had rescued a injured GI who had both his feet blown off by a grenade. Gave him first aid, carried him to a helicopter while under fire.

One album photo showed Hamilton with four others standing outside a primitive village house somewhere in a jungle. The photos were held down with corner tabs. Caryl popped the photo loose and looked on the back. There were first names scrawled in pencil. Was one of those GIs the man Hamilton rescued, Caryl wondered. Was that GI still alive? Like the Major, he'd now be in his sixties.

Other photos were troubling, GI's using their cigarette lighters to set fire to thatched roofs. Crying people who had little more than the clothes they stood in, watching their homes being destroyed. Then bodies. Women, even children. It was one of those wartime atrocities that happen in spite of the rules of war, as if war were some sort of a football game with penalties for off-sides or unnecessary roughness. There were also grisly close-ups of the dead. Hamilton's trophy shots..

Luckily the pictures were all black and white.

Those were taken before digital photography. Someone had carried a camera to record everything. There were only twelve photos in the album. Typically a roll of black and white film took thirty-six exposures. Had the rest not come out? Had they been thrown away as not good enough to put in an album? There might be film, negatives.

Were the pictures of the village being destroyed only one incident? Was the citation for the medal about some other place? Caryl would have to find that wounded GI, if he was still alive, and get his side of the story.

He looked up Major Hamilton's phone number in the Plaza directory and called. Arthur Hamilton should be in his father's apartment.

He was.

"This is Detective Fox. I need to see what's in your father's safety deposit box. We have the key."

"The key's not enough. Only people authorized can open the box. I'm not. The government and the banks are always worried that the heirs will help themselves to a stash of cash or something."

"Then call your father's lawyer. Frizbee. Let's all meet at the Umpqua bank and get that box open."

Arthur Hamilton made an appointment and called back. If they hurried they could get to the branch bank before it closed at 1:00.

They met in the lobby of the Rose Plaza a few feet from the bank. Frizbee had put on a suit for this occasion. It was an off the rack pin stripe of uncertain age with narrow lapels no longer in style. Frizbee needed a haircut and looked as seedy as his office.

Cynically Caryl assumed that the Frizbee's attendance would go down in the books as billable hours. Frizbee looked like he needed the money and could charge the Major's estate, whatever that might be.

The Umpqua was a one person branch bank whose customers were probably mainly Plaza residents and the staff. The name plate for the clerk said Jean. She looked to be in her mid twenties and wore her hair swept up and high, no makeup so she looked pale like she never got enough sunshine, not so unusual in rainy Portland.

She let the three men into the small vault room which had only a table and a single chair. After Frizbee identified himself as the executor of Major Hamilton's estate and Caryl Fox provided the key, the safety deposit box was unlocked and the slender steel box pulled out and set down at the table.

In the box Major Hamilton had stashed an old, gold wrist watch with a cracked glass. It might have been his own father's watch. There was also a ring with a small diamond which Arthur recognized as his mother's engagement ring. That was the only jewelry. The Major had worn a single gold band and a military ring which the medical examiner had removed and put in the Major's effects.

In a narrow, bank manila envelope typically used for stocks and bonds, there were several documents. One was a duplicate DD 214 discharge paper from the US Army. Another was the Major's birth certificate.

Someone else might have tucked away a diploma or two, a high school yearbook with photos, souvenirs like that. Apparently Major Hamilton either wasn't sentimental or with all the moves military folks made, they got lost.

What Arthur Hamilton hoped to find were adoption papers listing his birth mother's name, father unknown. What he found was something in Vietnamese which neither he nor Caryl could read. There was a yellowed foreign identity card with the faded picture of an infant. At that age, most babies looked alike. What came first? The surname or the first name? What looked like some sort of certificate looked official, but was in a foreign language, presumably Vietnamese. Instead of solving the mystery of Arthur Hamilton's origins, the contents of the safety deposit box created more.

What attracted Caryl Fox's attention was a film canister containing at least one roll of black and white negatives. With Arthur's permission Caryl held the negatives up to the light. "Can you take these to a shop and get prints made?"

Arthur held them up to the fluorescent light and shook his head. "I don't think many places still do black and white prints from negatives. Everything's digital now. Last time I ordered a print from an old negative it took two weeks. They send that stuff to a lab someplace."

"Maybe that's what they do in Syracuse. This is Portland. Let me try," Caryl suggested. "I think the precinct can get a rush job."

He agreed, though reluctantly.

"Thanks." Caryl bagged the canister as evidence and put it in his pocket, but not before it was duly noted on the deposit box inventory.

The box contained no money other than an envelope with a couple of foreign bank notes, probably Vietnamese money that no longer had any value other than sentimental. There was also a GI life insurance policy.

Arthur Hamilton was disappointed. "I was hoping there'd be a birth certificate for me."

Then there was an envelope marked "Last Will and Testament." Frizbee put it in the inside pocket of his jacket. "I need to make sure this is the same one I have at my office. Let's go there and check. Then we can read the will."

"We'll meet at your office," Caryl suggested, and followed Frizbee out the entrance. "You can ride with me, Arthur." He preferred to be on a first name basis when he conducted an interview.

They convened at Frizbee's downtown office. Frizbee was not much of a file clerk and had no secretary. He had some trouble locating his copy of

Major Hamilton's will, was satisfied that the copies were identical, and studied them before saying anything.

Finally he spread the document out on the table. It was only one sheet of paper. After the usual the formality, "I Aaron Hamilton, of sound mind and body, declare this to be my last will and testament. I am to be cremated and my cremains deposited in the National Cemetery in Portland. My GI life insurance policy will cover the costs."

Frizbee paused. "After the medical examiner releases his body you can see about his cremation. You'll need to contact the Veterans' Administration about the burial. But let's go on. 'I will my personal effects to my son Arthur. I want five thousand dollars to go to Vaughn Swenson, if he is still alive. The remainder of my cash accounts and investments are to go to the Portland chapter of the Vietnamese Orphan Society.'"

That was it, plain and simple. It was dated just after his wife had died and after they moved into the Rose Plaza. Hamilton's signature had been witnessed and notarized by Mrs. Grafton.

"No money?" Arthur asked. "Not that I expected any."

Frizbee wasn't surprised. "Retired military tend not to accumulate much wealth. There's his life insurance policy, of course. I suppose the bulk of his savings went into his move in fee at the Rose Plaza. He had a choice apartment."

Caryl Fox wasn't aware of how the Rose Plaza worked. Frizbee explained that it was a buy in place. You paid a lump sum on entry for a life time lease, but the apartment could not be inherited or sold. It wasn't part of the Major's estate.

"Dad hated the Communists, but I guess he had a soft spot for the Vietnamese people."

There was a pause while that thought sank in. Then Arthur asked no one in particular, "Who the hell is Vaughn Swenson?"

Caryl thought about the photos he had already seen in the so-called kill book. "There's a Vaughn named on the back of one of the pictures in his album. Could be an old army buddy. Might be the guy he rescued. Did he ever mention this orphan society to you?"

Arthur Hamilton shook his head. "Never. Like I said, we weren't on speaking terms after I called him a war criminal."

"Yet he adopted you."

"I guess that makes sense."

"It would, especially if he were your birth father."

Arthur's face showed remorse. "I wish I could find my birth mother. All this paper has is what looks like her name. I can't read Vietnamese."

Frizbee knew something about the Vietnam war. "Maybe she handed you over as a baby during the evacuation. Did you ever see the news clips? It was chaos."

Frizbee required a signature from Arthur Hamilton. Caryl consented to sign as a witness to the reading of the will. Frizbee mumbled something about a final bill. He reminded Arthur that Executors get a statutory commission based on the value of the estate.

Caryl was reminded that he still had his own GI life insurance policy and kept up the payments even though he had no beneficiaries other than his parents. As for Arthur Hamilton's problem, he had a suggestion. "Maybe the Orphan Society can help you.'

Caryl also wanted to talk to the Vietnamese Orphan Society. What pictures were on that roll of film? As for Vaughn Swenson, that was another lead to Major Hamilton's past.

Since Hamilton appeared to have no friends in Portland other than the now dead girl friend, he suspected that something in the Major's past was connected with his murder.

One thing certain: he did not want the murder of Major Hamilton to end up in Detective Casey's old file of cold cases. If that happened, he had failed.

Chapter nineteen

Caryl phoned J.J. and asked her to find out about the girl's parents. Her sister had not been appropriately shocked at the news of the murder. She was also not very forthcoming when talking to the police. Perhaps she was shielding her sister from a charge of prostitution. Not that a dead person could be charged, but her friends might be involved. In that neighborhood the police were seen as the enemy, not to be confided in.

There was more than one reason for not approving of her sister's profession. A hooker could make more money than a waitress, so there was that conflict, too. Jealousy. Nothing was simple.

A waitress might be yelled at, but not choked o death with her own panties..

Then there was the problem of Vaughn Swenson, disabled Vietnam veteran. Caryl hoped he could use his badge to get past the issue of patient confidentiality and find him.

Fortunately, the Portland VA hospital was just up the hill from the Rose Plaza. The hospital was a massive building connected to OHSU, the Oregon Health Sciences University, by a sky bridge. Marquam hill was a crowded conglomerate of buildings. The Shriners had their building, and there was the Dorenbecker children's hospital, too. There was a nursing school, library, annexes, parking garages, all stacked and connected. When the university overflowed the hill additional buildings were put on the waterfront of the Willamette River and connected by a Swiss built aerial tram that carried sixty people at a time over a maze of streets and the I-5 freeway.

The electric sign at the VA garage entrance indicated there were only twenty seven spaces left of the three hundred, but the garage had three levels, so it took some hunting. Caryl didn't want to occupy an emergency or handicapped spot. The space he squeezed into beside a huge four by four pickup truck was so tight he couldn't open the driver's side door and had to crawl over the equipment that cluttered the driver's compartment. Luckily he was skinny and limber enough to make it.

He took the elevator up to the main floor, crowded with the wages of war. Veterans of all ages and degrees of disability were waiting stoically on lounge chairs for their number to come up. They all looked poor. Some wore the dregs of uniforms. Many had baseball caps that identified their branch of service or the name of the ship they sailed on. A volunteer was playing popular tunes on the battered grand piano.

Of course, Caryl was a veteran, too, in spite of his short stint in the service. He had been at the VA hospital before for treatments related to his change. He had seen a couple of OHSU residents in their resident year, beautiful young women who were especially interested in him as an unusual case and an opportunity. There weren't that many transgender GIs. It had made him feel like a lab rat.

Caryl used his badge to jump the waiting line and get into the registration office. The clerk he saw was a disabled person, probably a veteran taking advantage of the VA hiring policy. The name tag hanging around his neck, first name George, had a number of pins and awards attached. He wore a gaudy Hawaiian shirt. A pair of crutches stood within reach of his office chair.

"I'm investigating the murder of Major Aaron Hamilton. He got the Silver Star for rescuing another GI who was wounded in Vietnam. The soldier's name was Vaughn Swenson. Lost both feet." Caryl had taken a quick photograph of the citation for Hamilton's silver star on his cell phone and showed it. "I need to contact Swenson if he's still alive."

The clerk studied the cell phone image. "I need his last four and date of birth."

They always asked for that. The last four digits of the social security number and date of birth were like pass words. Without providing that information you couldn't get medical treatment. "Don't have it."

"Then I can't help you."

Caryl flipped through more of the pictures on the cell phone. He had added all the photos in the kill album. He showed the one with the four GI's posing. "He's one of these men."

"You don't know which one?"

"I think he's the one on the right." Caryl paused, leaned over the desk and lowered his voice. "Come on, George. I know the clerks run the army. I bet you can find him. What about the details in the citation?"

The wrinkles around George's eyes deepened as he smiled. "You don't want me to give out any military secrets, Detective..."

"Caryl."

"Detective Caryl. Say, weren't you once private Carol? I seen your record before."

One couldn't keep a secret. Army clerks knew everything. "It's Caryl now, George. What about this Swenson?"

"I could run a data search on Vietnam vets who lost both feet and are named Swenson. Can't be a lot of them."

"I knew you could."

"We're pretty busy here, Detective. I'll see what I can find out on my break. You got a card?"

Caryl handed over one of his business cards. Detective Caryl Fox. Homicide. Portland Police."

George the clerk was impressed. "Could you fix a parking ticket?"

"I'm not in the traffic department. If you do murder, we might talk about it."

"I know a few administrators who might deserve it, but I don't do that. I'll phone you if I find anything."

"Thanks." Caryl stood up to go. "Nice shirt."

"I got twenty four of 'em."

Luckily the pickup truck that had been parked beside Caryl's squad car had pulled out and been replaced by a compact. He had no trouble getting back in.

Next? Find out about Long's parents. Maybe they knew something. From what he knew about Long, she didn't work the streets but had a regular list. She must have kept a ledger of her clients. She must have broken away from Tyrone Brown, grounds for revenge, but Brown had an alibi. There were other possibilities, clients beside Major Hamilton.

Then there was the orphans' organization mentioned in Hamilton's will. What was his connection?

Someone had to know something that would lead to his killer. Getting up to the twelfth floor of the Rose Plaza with its remote apartment took knowledge and planning. The murder had been premeditated, not one of those spur of the moment killings of a person who confronts a burglar in his house.

As for Arthur's birth mother, that was a search he'd have to do himself.

Chapter twenty

J.J. called him back at the precinct. She had talked with
Lotus Nguen and found out about her parents and called
them. As teenagers the Nguens had both been boat
people, part of that wave of immigrants after the
Vietnam War and met in a transit camp for
rehabilitation. Her father had first worked in a dry
cleaning business, then opened his own place on Barbur
Boulevard. It wasn't unusual for Vietnamese to open
restaurants or go into some service industry. Portland
had a lot of ethnic restaurants. As for dry cleaning, you
didn't have to know a lot of English to take an order for
removing food stains from a pair of pants. Had they
been Pakistani or Indian they might have bought a
motel. Tired of the Oregon rain, they sold the dry
cleaning business and moved to Texas.

Someone had to identify the body and arrange a
funeral. Long's father agreed to come. Mrs. Nguen was
in poor health, a heart and lung problem she said, from
breathing too much carbon tet cleaning fluid, but Mr.
Nguen could fly to Portland to identify his daughter. J.J.
told Mr. Nguen he could take the red line Max from the
airport and change to the Green Line They could meet
at a restaurant at the Town Center and go on from there
to the medical examiner's office.

Long's murder was J.J.'s case, but Caryl wanted to
be there for the meeting, too, two heads being better
than one. It was a long drive for Caryl from the precinct
to the Town Center, but driving around Portland's
congestion was part of the job even if you could resort
to the flashing lights and siren of a patrol car. Caryl was
getting tired of running around and not keen on another
visit to the land of the corpses.

He was putting on his hooded rain jacket to leave the precinct when the desk phone rang. It was the crime lab with a breakthrough.

"We got a fingerprint off the tape used to bind the Major to his chair."

"Have you got a match?"

"I'm running it through the national database now. I can say it's not one of the prints we already found in the apartment. Not the major's, the hooker's, or the maid."

The fact that the Major was a recluse helped. Nobody came to visit but his Asian girl.

"Call me on my cell phone as soon as you get a match. His killer may have split."

Caryl got delayed in traffic on McLaughlin. He hadn't been to the Town Center often. As a Portland detective most of his work was in the city. Town Center was in Clackamas county. The parking lot was enormous and it was raining again. This time he took one of the dozen handicapped spots and went in search of the restaurant J.J. had picked out.

The restaurant J.J. chose was also a bakery. She didn't like some restaurant smells, especially burger joints smelling of burnt beef patties. As he came in the door he was struck by the familiar mixture of pastry and bread fragrances. Besides the high, glass display counter there were tables when you could drink your coffee and savor a croissant.

He spotted J.J. at the back with a small, Asian man who looked to be in poor health. He wore glasses with built in hearing aids. Though Caryl had heard that Vietnamese girls were beautiful, as Long was, apparently it didn't apply equally to the men. Long's father looked like gravity had done its work on his cheeks, chin, and throat. He might be diabetic.

His wheeled carryon was parked beside his chair with the PDX baggage label.

At least Caryl didn't have to be the one who broke the news that the Nguen's daughter had been murdered.

J.J. had done that. Mr. Nguen's expression was frozen in an attitude of grief.

J.J. had ordered coffees. Caryl took a pass, concentrated on questions that didn't get into Long's business. Maybe her father didn't know she was hooking.

Mr. Nguen was one of those people who spo0ke only when spoken to. He was not a chatty person, possibly hampered by his poor hearing. Getting information out of him was as tedious as trying to pull a splinter out of a foot. All Mr. Nguen knew was Long had briefly been a pole dancer at a gentleman's club on 128th street. She hadn't liked being stared at and the remarks the customers made. She was not that athletic and if she slipped or fell some men jeered. He didn't know Long had a practice pole in the apartment she shared with her sister.

As for boy friends, Long had never introduced any of them to her parents. Texas was too far away from Portland for close family relationships. She had mentioned the Major, that he wanted to marry her, but she said he was too old for her. They had never met him.

Putting together all that information took two cups of coffee and patience.

Mr. Nguen had not seen the selfie photograph and didn't know what the Major looked like. Caryl had the folder of photos with him and showed the picture. Of course he did not show any of the crime scene shots. Nguen was not aware of the murder of Major Hamilton.

It was a dead end. Caryl was not surprised. There were always leads that went nowhere. What he needed was one that was real. "What about the Vietnamese Orphan Society?"

"Oh, yes." Mr. Nguen nodded. "They meet every month."

"If we go to a meeting, who should we talk to?"

To J.J.'s chagrin, Mr. Nguen deferred to Caryl. If was one of those situations where the woman was not, to his mind, in charge. Nguen didn't see the irony of Caryl being transgender. He gave Caryl a name and the address.

Caryl mulled over the information he had. Hamilton had left his estate to the orphan society. His interest hadn't ended with the adoption of Arthur. The meeting with Mr. Nguen had not been a total bust after all. One had to pursue every possible thread.

He would have to visit the Orphan Society web site.

They still had to make that necessary identification of Long's body. Caryl had enough of the smell of formalin and death. In deference to J.J. he let her be in charge of that unpleasantness while he waited in the parking lot outside the medical examiner's office in the patrol car, the engine running, the radio lively with police calls. The rain hammered on the roof and the hood of the patrol car.

J.J. would drive Mr. Nguen to the daughter's apartment. She helped him into the back seat of the unmarked. Before getting in she walked over to Caryl's car and tapped the window. "You getting squeamish about visiting bodies?"

He ducked that one. "The crime lab called. They found a fingerprint on the tape used to bind Major Hamilton. Tracking it now. There might be some DNA evidence."

J.J. was more interested in Long Nguen. "Maybe you'll get lucky." The Hamilton murder was his case. She got in the unmarked and drove off with Mr. Nguen. It was one thing to talk about his daughter's murder over the phone. Seeing the body was traumatic. The old man sat crumpled in grief in the back seat.

Caryl needed to get lucky. It was a matter of self-esteem. His other cases had not been a challenge. The murder of Major Hamilton was like a blister on his heel. Every time he took a step, it hurt.

The Major had been a decorated war veteran. Caryl was a veteran, too, so to speak. Caryl had not been to Vietnam and hardly knew how to find it on a map, but they had both worn the uniform and taken the pledge.

Like it or not, it was like a brotherhood of those who served.

As he drove back into Portland he felt that the fingerprint might just solve the case. Fingerprints weren't always conclusive but they helped. He had to present the prosecutor with enough evidence for a grand jury. If the print was only on file...

Chapter twenty-one

Of course, a fingerprint was not enough. He didn't know where the tape came from, and anyone might have handled it, even a hardware store clerk. We leave our fingerprints and DNA everywhere. A fingerprint on the tape didn't necessarily put the owner of the print at the crime scene at all. Still, it was a lead.

The Portland FBI were still embarrassed by the case of the partial print found on a bomb fragment in Spain after the attack on the subway that killed so many people. The finger print allegedly linked to a Moslem lawyer in Portland. He was innocent, but the arrest had nearly destroyed the man's life and ended with a settlement for damages. You had to be careful.

Those expensive settlements of law suits against the Portland police were not in the budget. Caryl was afraid of making a mistake.

Whose fingerprint was on the tape? He would have to wait.

In the meantime there was a shooting outside a night club in Old Town. This one had witnesses and CCT evidence. Cut and dried. The perp had even confessed.

The murder of Long Nguen was tougher, no witnesses, no CCT, hardly any evidence. That was the kind of case that might take years to solve and then only if the killer, already in jail for something else, bragged to a cell mate about it.

The clerk at the VA hospital came through.

"I found your Viet vet," he said over the phone. "Swenson. You're in luck. He lives in Salem, right here in Oregon." He gave Caryl the address and phone number.

"Great. I have to see him."

"You're a lucky guy, Detective. I called him."

Caryl would have preferred to make the call himself. "I hope you didn't tell him why I wanted to contact him."

"No. I just reminded him about his appointment here at the VA this week. He'll be coming in on the shuttle. He doesn't drive."

"When is his appointment?"

"Friday afternoon, but the shuttle comes in early. They usually have several guys and have to get here early enough for the first one, then stay until the last appointment is over. It's usually an all day deal."

Caryl had seen the various shuttles parked outside the hospital. The Portland hospital was the main VA facility for the entire state of Oregon. There were clinics, like one in Newport, but if you needed specialty treatment, it meant some long drives, like from Bend and other locations in Eastern Oregon. Geographically Oregon was like two states, the rainy forests west of the Cascades and the high rural desert to the east.

Luckily for Swenson, Salem was little more than an hour's drive down the I-5 corridor.

Caryl would have to wait until Friday.

That was just as well, for he didn't expect the prints from that roll of 35 mm black and white film to be ready before then. He asked if there was anyone who worked in the Precinct who could make prints. With most people having switched to digital photography, only a hobbyist or serious art photographer still worked with film, all those chemicals and a darkroom. Had the film been color, there might be a drug store that could take the order. He learned that photo shops, which had once done a thriving business in developing and printing, now got perhaps a few rolls a week to develop. The equipment that developed film now did only color. Black and white was old technology.

Fortunately, someone at the precinct knew a vetted photographer who still did black and white prints in his basement darkroom. Caryl ordered two 8x10 prints of each negative on the roll. It was going to be expensive. He had to file a work order and hoped it wouldn't be rejected.

In the meantime, maybe there'd be a match on the fingerprint.

He checked the web site for the Orphans. When did they meet next, and who were the officers?

Chapter twenty-two

The web site for the Vietnamese Orphans Association had a history page. They met once a month at a neighborhood community center on Sandy Boulevard on the east side of Portland. Though the wave of immigrants after Vietnam had subsided, adoptions of orphans still took place. It was under strict control of the present Communist government. The adoption process was lengthy and expensive. On the other hand, even though hard currency was welcome, the Vietnamese government didn't want to appear to be in the business of selling babies. They also needed to know for certain that the birth mother agreed to the adoption or could not be found. There had been a few cases when the mother, once in improved circumstances, recanted, wanted her child back. Custody cases were traumatic for all parties, especially the child.

Then there were those current American citizens, children who had been adopted, and wanted to locate their birth mothers. That was the category Arthur Hamilton fell into. If he wanted to locate his birth mother, that was his business, not Caryl's.

Caryl had his own reasons for wanting to contact the group. The fact that the bulk of Hamilton's estate went to them, not his own son was only one of them. Being the bearer of such good tidings would give him an entrée. How much was Major Hamilton involved? Did he actually go to any of the meetings? Was there resentment that a retired US Army Major wanted to be involved? Or was he incognito and his bequest a surprise?

Arthur Hamilton had said his father was a war criminal, good reason not to reveal his concern for the orphans. It sounded to Caryl like a guilty conscience. That might be what was behind the major's PTSD.

But war was war. There was, as the Pentagon described them, collateral damage. It was a euphemism for carnage, the deaths of civilians, women, children, and the elderly. Caryl had heard that the co-pilot of the Enola Gay that dropped the atomic bomb on Hiroshima, Japan was so overcome with guilt that he joined a monastery. The pictures of the burned victims was too much for his conscience. Did the photo of the naked Vietnamese girl burned by napalm affect the pilot who dropped the bombs? Was every veteran torn by guilt?

Americans were not Afghans whose culture relished fighting. They were not Germans who saw Jews as vermin and had no revulsion about murdering them. If Americans had a lust for violence it was sublimated into a love of football. You didn't kill the other team or take down the spectators as collateral damage.

Caryl hadn't thought about collateral damage when he enlisted. He was interested in the signing bonus and the GI Bill. Now he had the murder of Major Hamilton to mull over. Was that a consequence that came back, like a World War II bomb that lay buried in the rubble of Berlin only to blow up when disturbed decades later?

Was it mere speculation on Caryl's part, or was he really getting into the personality of the dead Major? How well did we know anybody? Did he, for example, really know J.J.? They had a good working relationship, but they didn't eat together. They didn't even go out for a beer. She took no alcohol. He didn't know if her parents were also Moslems or if she had converted. It was none of his business.

Caryl decided that the best way to get the pulse of that Orphans' Association was to attend a meeting and see who they were. If Frizbee hadn't already informed them of the bequest, he might personally give them the news if only to see how they reacted when they learned who gave the association the money. Some people would be glad to get any donation. Others might feel it was tainted.

Had the Major hoped to buy redemption?

When Caryl arrived at the precinct the next morning, he brought a box of surplus pastry from his a landlord the baker to share around the precinct office. It was deliberate attempt to win the favor of his sometimes hostile co-workers on the Police force.

The tactic was not as successful as he hoped. Living above the Multnomah village bakery, his clothes were permeated with the smell—he would prefer fragrance—of yeast.

When he handed the carton of baked goods to the secretary instead of thanks, he got "What are you baking this time, Fox?"

He tried to ignore it. Even when he was a woman the only thing he ever baked was a tray of brownies out of a Duncan Hines mix. "Looks like jelly donuts. No refunds if you don't like them."

The first time he brought something it was a pleasant surprise. Lately the uniforms revealed they had gourmet tastes in donuts. Day old didn't cut it.

One of the older cops made a point of taking one bite and conspicuously tossing the rest into a waste basket.

Maybe Caryl should carry some kibbles in his pocket for the police dogs. They were always grateful even though their handlers didn't want competition. The dogs weren't trained to be friendly pets.

It was hard to be accepted. Before the change he resented guys staring at his boobs. Now he was surreptitiously regarded as a freak. He wouldn't ever be one of the guys, welcome to go for a beer at a bar.

The Portland bar scene was broken down by preferences. Caryl did not go to gay bars, for the gays didn't accept transgenders. If he wanted to nurse a cold one he had to do it in his apartment. It wasn't much fun to drink alone in front of trash TV shows.

The black and white prints were on his desk in a heavy manila envelope. Attached was a bill for a shocking three hundred and sixty dollars, five dollars a print. He sat down in Detective Casey's creaky desk chair, careful not too lean too far back, and opened the envelope. This better be worth the expense.

He spread the prints out on the desk in what he thought might be chronological order. One look and he lost his appetite for pastry. Now he thought he understood why the pictures hadn't been included in the Major's kill book. They were incriminating evidence.

He looked up Major Hamilton's phone number in the Rose Plaza directory and dialed. Arthur Hamilton might still be in the twelfth floor apartment.

Chapter twenty-three

He was. Detective Fox went right to the point. "I have prints from that roll of negatives we found in your father's safety deposit box. Want to come down to the precinct to look at them?"

Arthur Hamilton was reluctant. "I'm packing up his stuff. Can't you come here?"

Since Arthur was not a suspect, Caryl couldn't force him to come downtown. Caryl sighed. "I'll be right over. It's not pretty." To be honest, looking at Casey's file cabinet of cold cases wasn't pretty, either. It was depressing, like an accusation of inability or incompetence. Maybe he should get a vase and some flowers to brighten up this windowless office.

When Caryl reached the top floor of the Rose Plaza tower he saw that the apartment across from Major Hamilton's was still being remodeled. The Mexican plasterers and Philippine painters were gone. Now it was the carpet phase, a crew of two who turned out to be Ukrainians complete with knee pads. They emerged from the freight elevator with a roll of carpeting and were grateful that the apartment they were working on was so close by.

The carpet was to be installed without a pad under it. Caryl knew something about carpeting and saw that this was pretty cheap stuff. Since the average age of the Rose Plaza tenants was eighty-six, there was no point in installing a twenty year carpet. The contractor certainly was being international in his hiring, providing jobs for recent immigrants.

Caryl introduced himself, showed his badge, wanted to know the names of the two men, had they been in the apartment at the time the Major was murdered? They were Sergei and Misha, and no they had not. They moved from job to job as needed. Other apartments were being remodeled on the seventh floor.

As that know-everything Ms. Seller had explained to him, it was the policy of the Rose Plaza to remodel every vacant apartment as the previous tenants died. New lease holders got to specify colors, molding, carpeting, etc. within the limits of the basic floor plans. The constant remodeling kept the Rose Plaza up to date and fresh though it had been built in the 1950's.

Arthur Hamilton opened the door for Caryl. Even though the Major had not been a collector of bric-a-brac, his son was amassing a number of packing boxes of his father's stuff. He had already removed the contents of the storage locker. "Most of this is going to the Goodwill," Arthur explained. "I sure don't want any of it. It's not worth the cost of shipping it to Syracuse."

Caryl held up the envelope of photos. "Where can we spread these out?"

"On the dinette table."

It was a table for two with a Formica top and two bent wood chairs. Caryl moved the chairs so they were side by side. Psychologically, side by side sitting was less confrontational. This was not an interrogation.

Arthur Hamilton paled when he saw the photographs. "I can see why Dad didn't want these in his kill book. They're too gruesome. How many bullets did it take to kill a baby, anyway?"

Caryl pulled another print to the center of the display. "I think this is the worst." It depicted a Vietnamese prisoner tied to a tree. His face was contorted in fear and agony. A GI in a muddy uniform had used his combat knife to cut open the prisoner's chest.

There were three pictures in the sequence. In one the American was eating, or pretending to eat, a piece of the prisoner's liver. In the last, the camera had caught the moment when the man's brains were blown out. A similar shot of a prisoner being executed had won the photographer a Pulitzer prize and epitomized the brutality of the Vietnam war almost as vividly as the famous shot of the screaming little girl burned by Napalm.

Caryl had seen those historical photos at one time or another, but out of the context of the daily news reports the American public had been subjected to on the dinner hour news. No wonder Americans had turned against the war.

Arthur Hamilton turned to Caryl. "Who are the men in these pictures?"

"I think one is the man your father rescued under fire that got him the Silver Star medal. His name is Swenson. Lives in Salem."

Arthur shook his head. He was shocked and disgusted. "This other picture. That's my father. He was still a lieutenant then."

Arthur Hamilton was obviously upset. Caryl apologized. "I just needed a confirmation."

"My father was a war criminal."

"But you're not."

"God no. I never served."

Served was an expression used by everyone in relation to military service. People who found out that Caryl was a veteran sometimes thanked him for his service as if he'd done something heroic.

"Are you a veteran, Detective?"

Caryl didn't know exactly how to reply. "I was in the army briefly. Got a medical discharge."

Arthur looked at him, studied his face. "What for?"

"I needed a sex change."

Eyebrows lifted. "Oh."

"Does that bother you?"

Arthur had momentarily forgotten the war photos. He shook his head. "I couldn't care less. Just so you don't eat people."

Caryl gathered up the photos. "I had two sets made of these. Do you want one?"

"Never."

"Thanks for your time." Caryl got up to leave.

"Does that help your investigation?"

"It helps me know the Major, who he was. I'm going to talk to Swenson, so this helps me understand him, too."

Had this visit to Arthur Hamilton brought Caryl any closer to solving the murder? Or was it just another dead end?

Across the hall he looked in at the Ukrainians. The Major was killed between Friday night and the following Sunday. He asked the Ukrainians, "Do you do remodeling on Saturdays or Sundays?"

They didn't.

They had not been there at the time the Major was murdered. Had anyone else? Apparently the remodels went in stages as each phase was done by other members of the crew. He had met the Mexican sheet rock team. Who had been in the apartment on Friday who might have seen something unusual? There was so little traffic at that end of the twelfth floor corridor, any activity might be noticed.

Caryl took the freight elevator down to the first floor and passed the administration offices. In the breezeway where he could get a strong cell signal he called J.J. "J.J. Did you ask Long's sister if she kept a ledger or journal of her customers?"

"Yes. She had three regulars. The Major was Friday night. She had another on Thursday and, would you believe? On Wednesday she had a minister."

"I wonder if she prayed before or after sex."

"Maybe she called them prayer meetings."

"We have to interview those men. When the selfie was published, one of the men might have been jealous or vindictive. Let's see if we can find them." He remembered that Long's cell phone was blocked. "Did she list their real names?"

"No. But their phone numbers are in her book."

"Let's get them."

Chapter Twenty-four

That wasn't difficult. Fortunately both men had used their main numbers that could be traced to their addresses. They hadn't gone to the trouble to use a burn phone, one of those disposable off the shelf anonymous phones that could be discarded. Long's so-called clients were not that sophisticated.

Both Caryl and J.J. wanted to arrange a face to face interview with each "client." They met in the lobby of the bank building at Sixth and Burnside. Caryl brought his file with the selfie and other photos. Up they went to the twentieth floor.

While in the privacy of the elevator Caryl gave J.J. a quick glimpse of the prints from the negatives found in the Major's safety deposit box. If he expected J.J. to be shocked he was disappointed. She had been exposed to so many gruesome crime scenes and bodies that she was calloused and unmoved. At least they were in black and white, not vivid bleeding color. In person, corpses smelled.

Since the murder of Long Nguen was her case, J.J. would lead the questioning. Because Caryl felt the publication of the selfie of them both had precipitated her murder, he was sure there was some connection with the Major.

Their quarry for the first interview was an insurance executive, Bartholomew Hawkins. His receptionist was a babe who might fit in well in the offices of Playboy. She was blond, perfumed, and underdressed for the job in a blouse with cleavage and a skirt just long enough to be legal. Obviously Hawkins liked his women. As a woman Caryl would have been envious, but as a man he was objectively unimpressed. She was not his type, but then, who was? Sexy babes didn't turn him on. If anything he had become androgynous. The transition to being a man was hard enough. He had trouble imagining having sex with anyone.

Caryl had no trouble imagining Hawkins' hot receptionist getting humped over her boss's desk. If so, why did he need the services of Long Nguen?

The receptionist would have put them off, saying Bart--she was on a first name basis—was busy and did they have an appointment?

J.J.'s badge got them admitted.

Bart (Bartholomew) Hawkins turned out to be surprisingly short. His hair was an unnatural auburn color and might have been a wig. Seeing the man himself Caryl came to a different conclusion about the choice of receptionist. Bartholomew might have her as compensation for his own sense of sexual inadequacy. That might also fit in with his use of Long Nguen. A guy like that might have difficulty getting a date, often the case of intimidated men shorter than their women. Long, being Vietnamese, was a small woman.

J.J. got right to the point. "Detective Caryl Fox and I are investigating the murder of a miss Long Nguen."

Hawkins shook his head, confused. "I don't know anyone of that name."

Caryl dug into his folder for the selfie. "You might know her as Lotus. Maybe you saw this photo in the newspaper?"

Without looking at the picture Hawkins explained, "I only read the Wall Street Journal."

J.J. was unimpressed by his choice of newspapers. "She wouldn't be on the financial pages, Mr. Hawkins. You are on Long Nugent's list of clients. You are the Thursday guy. Did you see her every Thursday?"

Caught, he had to own up. "When I'm in town. What did you say about murder?" The expression on his face was a mixture of confusion, pain, shock, and maybe guilt.

Caryl explained, "She was found strangled at Rocky Ridge."

J.J. corrected him. "Rocky Butte. It's a lookout in Northeast Portland."

"I don't know where that is."

"But you do admit you know the sex worker who went by the name of Lotus."

He admitted he did. "Sex therapist. That's not illegal, is it?"

J.J. shook her head like where is this guy from? "Maybe if this were Nevada, but for all its weirdness the sex trade is still illegal in Portland."

"Are you going to arrest me for consorting with a prostitute? If so you'll have to arrest half the men in Portland."

"The jails are already full, Mr. Hawkins, but we could probably use the fine money."

Caryl broke in. "We're not concerned with your off duty recreation. Long Nguen was strangled. Maybe you did it?"

"No way." Bartholomew looked at his phone. "If you're accusing me, maybe I should call my lawyer."

J.J. wasn't ready for that. "Not at this preliminary stage."

Bartholomew leaned forward and lowered his voice. "Lotus was just a regular fuck. She was discreet. Came to my condo. No sleazy motel rooms. No drugs." He paused and frowned. "I'm sorry she'd dead."

He didn't seem that sorry. There was plenty of competition in the Portland sex trade. Long Nguen would be easily replaced. She was just a disposable commodity.

J.J. had enough. She passed her business card to Bartholomew, which he left laying on the desk. "We'll be talking with you again later."

Caryl wasn't finished. "What about the other face in this selfie? Know that man? Major Hamilton?"

"No."

"He was murdered, too. Lived on the top floor of the Rose Plaza."

"Oh, so that who it was!" He seemed genuinely surprised. "My aunt told me about it. Had his liver cut out or something like that."

The liver detail had not bee publicized. "How do you know that?"

"My aunt lives at the Rose Plaza. We had dinner the other night."

J.J. was exasperated. "How did your aunt find out?"

"Some old lady who lives there, always wears a beret. She came over to the table and told us all about it."

Caryl sighed. Mrs. Seller was a busy body and a motor mouth. "What floor does your aunt live on?"

"She's on the eleventh floor."

"Do you take the freight elevator?"

"There's a freight elevator? I didn't know."

Now, as Sherlock might have said, but never did according to Conan Doyle experts, the game was afoot. Caryl asked, "Did you visit your aunt last Saturday or Sunday?"

"I join her at the breakfast forum on Saturday morning. She likes the bacon and sausages at the buffet."

J.J. grimaced. Bacon and sausages were definitely not halal.

"So you are familiar with the building."

Hawkins didn't get it. "Sure. Why?"

"Ever been on the twelfth floor?"

He hadn't been, or so he said.

Caryl held up the selfie. "And you never saw the Major before just now?"

"Nope."

Had Hawkins encountered the Major or his killer in the elevator that might have been a lucky break. His case seemed to provide no luck at all.

As they left the building J.J. was fuming. "That bitch."

It was not a word Caryl would use. "You mean Mrs. Seller. As for Hawkins, he might have a motive to kill

Long. She could have been black mailing him. We didn't ask if he was married."

J.J. nodded. "Then our next step with Hawkins is to check his bank records for regular large withdrawals and Long's bank to see if she made corresponding deposits."

"Right. And let's find out what Hawkins drives. We have three patrol cars with license plate readers. Might be useful to see where his car has been. If it's a new model luxury car I bet it has a GPS built in that tracks it."

"You mean like the car the Boston bombers hijacked and led the police right to them."

"Exactly. Maybe his car was at Rocky Butte."

Caryl was feeling sorry for Long, alias Lotus. It wasn't clear what her relationship had been with Tyrone Brown who was now sitting at the Canadian border on a parole violation and a charge of human trafficking. Caryl didn't rule out the possibility that Brown contracted with someone to kill her. "Too bad about Long. She wasn't an 82nd street hooker. What hookers have to be afraid of are the serial killers who think they must purge the streets of sin."

"And easy prey."

"I guess she thought she was high class with those regular clients. Didn't help."

J.J. agreed. They had reached the street. "Speaking of clients, our next stop is Mr. Wednesday."

Chapter twenty-five

The street sign outside the Lutheran church said "Hate the sin, love the sinner." That depended on your definition of love, as in making love. Caryl found the irony amusing.

J.J. had confiscated Long's appointment book. The phone number belonged to the church but the client's name was just "pastor." So who was the pastor at the Lutheran church?

The church was not locked. Inside, the sanctuary was Spartan, no elaborate decorations or Stations of the Cross you might find in a Catholic cathedral. The altar had no statue of Jesus, just a simple, wooden cross. The board beside the pulpit carried the numbers of the hymns scheduled for the next service, or the last one.

The office was at the back with a name plate, Hokanson. J.J. knocked.

They were greeted by a grey-haired man of uncertain age. He was dressed in a threadbare, black suit that said a pastor's lifestyle was not wealthy. His face was thin and he had a scratch on his left cheek only partly covered by a plastic strip. "Can I help you?"

"You can help us," J.J said, showing her badge. "This is Detective Caryl Fox and I'm J.J. We're investigating a murder and hope you might be of some help."

"Murder?"

Caryl showed the selfie. "Actually two murders."

Before he could say more Hokanson blanched. He recognized Long. "I warned her."

"The girl went by a working name of Lotus, but her real name was Long Nguen. She's Vietnamese."

Hokanson nodded. "I know, but who is the man in the picture?"

"Major Hamilton."

J.J. added, "He was her Friday client. According to her appointment book, you were her Wednesday regular."

Hokanson swallowed before speaking. "Yes, I saw her on Wednesdays."

"For sex?"

Hokanson actually blushed. "Well, not at first. I saw her ad as a sex therapist in Willamette Week. I thought I would counsel her."

Caryl raised his eyebrows. "Counsel her?"

J.J. had another word for it. "You mean save her soul."

"Well, yes. That's what church business is all about."

"Why Wednesdays?" J.J. asked. "Couldn't she just come to church on Sundays?"

"Well," Pastor Hokanson, admitted, "It was more than that. I needed some sex therapy myself."

"So it was a two way street," Caryl suggested. "I save your soul and you give me great sex."

Hokanson looked down sheepishly at the blotter on his desk. "When you put it that way."

J.J. was taking notes. "So who paid who? Did she tithe, or did you pay her for services?"

"I paid her."

"How much?"

Hokanson looked guilty. "A hundred dollars a session."

Caryl didn't think, by the cut of the Pastor's clothes that he could afAudi a hundred dollar hooker. "So did you pay her out of church funds?"

Hokanson squared his shoulders. "The church supports several charities."

J.J. took a breath to control herself. "I'll take that as a yes. So paying Long for sex was a charitable contribution in your crusade against prostitution?"

Caryl added, "I wonder how your congregation would see it. If she exposed you, you could be fired or defrocked or whatever Lutherans do."

No answer.

J.J. persisted. "Did she threaten to expose you? Demand more money?"

Hokanson paled and nodded. "That might have been possible."

Caryl got to the point. "So did you kill her to keep her quiet?"

"Of course not. I didn't know she was dead until you showed me that picture. How did it happen?"

J.J. looked him in the eye. "She was found strangled up on Rocky Butte."

Hokanson crumpled. He started to cry, his face contorted with grief. "I failed. I warned her. I tried to save her."

J.J. gave him her card. "You can call me any time if you can think of anything that might lead us to her killer."

As they turned to leave Caryl asked "What happened to your cheek?"

Hokanson touched the plastic strip. "I was cutting down blackberry bushes in the back yard. A branch snapped back and caught me.".

Blackberry bushes, not native to the Pacific North West, grew like persistent, aggressive weeds. Only Llamas or goats had mouths tough enough to eat them.

Outside the church J.J. could hardly contain herself. "Hypocrite! What a phony."

"Twisted logic," Caryl said.

"I can't stand it. That's why I converted to Islam."

"I wondered about that."

"Why can't you men keep it in your pants?" Then she hesitated apologetically, gestured toward Caryl's crotch. "Sorry, I guess you don't have anything in there."

"I don't want to talk about it."

She was genuinely sorry. "I apologize. None of my business."

Caryl put his arm around J.J.'s shoulder. "We both have our own problems."

J.J. cringed. She was not used to being touched.

Standing outside their respective cars, Caryl asked, "Where do we go from here?"

"I don't think Hokanson's our man. What was his accent? Minnesota?"

"Maybe he was one of those Norwegian bachelor farmers who found God."

J.J. consulted her notes. "We'll follow up on Hawkins, bank records and such. What about you?"

"I'm seeing a disabled veteran on Friday. The man the Major rescued. He's coming up from Salem."

Back in his apartment above the bakery in Multnomah Village Caryl took a shower as if it were a baptism to purge himself of the sin around him. He had rejected the old life. Studying his image in the steamy mirror he looked at the scars of the double mastectomy. The VA surgeons had made no effort to make his chest look normal. The nipples were gone, not moved to look natural. There was no reconstructive work like a cancer victim might want. The operation had been the confirmation of his decision. There was no turning back. Did he have regrets? Sometimes. Life was complicated.

He had rejected one gender, but could not be 100 percent the other. As such he was neither fish nor fowl. As such, he was an outcast. Sex and gender were not the same. You could change gender and not have sex.

Chapter Twenty-six

Caryl had to be at the VA hospital at eight o'clock Friday morning to meet the shuttle from Salem. There were six veterans aboard and had to arrive in time for the earliest appointment. The van, highly decorated with the stars and stripes, was driven by a volunteer veteran who wore a heavily emblazed jacket that left no doubt of his service in Vietnam. Like many veterans, the most exciting or traumatic period in their life was their military service. Everything before or since paled.

If was easy to spot Vaughn Swenson. He was the last one out of the van and struggled with crutches. Whether by design there was no attempt to conceal the fact that he had lost both feet. They'd been replaced by mechanical prosthesis. Swenson's balance was poor and it took him an awkward moment while he straightened up and adjusted the crutches. His facial expression read unrelenting pain and suffering.

He was poorly dressed in faded blue jeans and an old field jacket. Caryl was surprised that Swenson could still be wearing his original uniform jacket. Usually men put on weight over the years. He might have found a duplicate in a military supply store. Perhaps wearing a vintage field jacket was a badge of honor, like the desert colored cammies some Iraqi vets wore. Maybe they didn't own civilian clothes or wanted the world to know where they had served.

Caryl had not kept his own army uniform. It was, after all, a woman's uniform and no longer appropriate. His medical discharge, though not dishonorable or general, was still nothing he waned to remember or brag about. He was grateful to possess a vet's ID card that got him medical care even though he was not defined as disabled.

"Vaughn Swenson?" he asked when his quarry had got his balance and looked up with some apprehension toward the revolving door. With crutches and prosthesis, every movement was a challenge.

"That's me. What's left anyway."

"I'm Detective Caryl Fox. I'm investigating a murder."

"What murder?"

"Major Hamilton. Aaron Hamilton."

Swenson was surprised, but recovered. "Oh, that Hamilton! I read about it in the Oregonian. I didn't know he was still alive. What's it got to do with me?"

"I thought you might tell me something about the time he saved your life. Why don't we go inside?"

They made their way through the revolving door which was big enough for a couple of wheelchairs. When they emerged into the crowded lobby Swenson hesitated, swallowed, and took a deep breath.

Caryl recognized the man's anxiety. "This is too crowded. Maybe we can find a quiet place to talk. When is your appointment?"

"Not until ten o'clock."

"We can have a cup of coffee in the café. Did you have breakfast?"

Swenson didn't look like he could afAudi a cup of coffee. "You buyin?"

"You're guest of the Portland Police."

"I ain't had breakfast yet. Had to leave early."

"Find yourself a quiet corner and I'll bring you something. Pancakes and sausage OK?"

"Sure." Swenson turned to Caryl and gave him the grateful look of a beggar who just scored a free meal. "Make the coffee black, no cream."

Caryl understood. The man was already institutionalized. He knew Swenson lived in a group home, an alternative to being a homeless Vietnam vet.

Group homes had rules, like no drugs or alcohol. You ate what you got.

Caryl bought the man two pancakes, sausage, and coffee, balanced the tray while holding his file of photos. He checked out using his police debit card and found Swenson tucked into a quiet corner of the café. He didn't buy coffee for himself, but got a cup of ice water in case he got dry mouth from his own nervousness about talking to a real disabled vet.

Caryl covered the next minutes with disarming small talk about how Swenson liked Salem, the group home, anything except what he had come for. He wasn't sure how to proceed. Finally, he broached the subject of Major Hamilton.

"Did you know Hamilton got the Silver Star for rescuing you?"

A shake of the head.

"What was your rank at the time?"

"Corporal. Hamilton was a snot nosed new lieutenant."

"So you didn't like him?"

"Nobody did. He was trying to prove himself, showing off, being macho. The rest of us just wanted to survive." Swenson sipped his coffee, had trouble holding the cup steady. "He cost me my feet."

"Can you tell me about the incident?"

Swenson took a bite of his last sausage and concentrated on chewing. "We were in this little Viet Kong village, just a few hooch houses. Hamilton asked one of the guys to take pictures he could send home to brag about. Then he set fire to a couple of them. Naturally the gooks got upset."

"I guess I would, too."

"Except someone started shooting and Hamilton went nuts."

Now Swenson looked down at his plate at the little puddle of syrup left beside the last bit of pancake. He had lost his appetite.

"I have the photos that were taken at the time." Caryl reached for his folder. He was particularly interested in the one showing the torture. He slipped it out.

Swenson's eyes opened wide with a recollection of fear.

The picture showed a deranged Hamilton carving a Vietnamese man's chest.

Swenson was now shaking. "That's him!"

"Who?" Caryl thought, Hamilton. The proof of a war crime that his son was so angry about.

"The kid!" Swenson pointed to a little boy half hidden in the shrubbery. "He was screaming for his papa. Then he disappeared. He must have sounded the alarm, because that triggered an ambush. We thought the village was unprotected. It was a trap…"

At that Swenson choked, bent over the side of his chair, vomited, and fell face down in a seizure.

The noise of the falling chair got everyone's attention. People in the café turned to look. One or two men jumped up and ran out. Caryl stood, not knowing what do to. Was it epilepsy?

He had never been present when someone had a seizure. What were you supposed to do? Keep the person from biting their tongue or swallowing it?

If someone had pulled a gun, Caryl would have known how to react, but this was a surprise.

The PA system announced some sort of code and in moments several orderlies rushed in, spotted Swenson on the floor and saw Caryl standing confused, holding the file of photos.

In a minute or two a gurney was rolled in and several staff members tried to get Swenson onto it. A bystander handed them his crutches.

One of the six men who had been on the Salem shuttle approached Caryl. "What happened? "

"I showed him a photograph and he flipped out.""

"Who the hell are you?"

"I'm Detective Caryl Fox. I'm investigating a murder."

"Whatever the fuck you did, detective, you triggered the man's PTSD." He spotted the file in Caryl's hand. "What did you show him?"

Numb, Caryl showed the torture photo.

"Jesus Christ, man. You can't do that to these guys. You've set Swenson back for months."

Caryl gulped. "I didn't know."

"Somebody should have your badge for this. That's incredibly insensitive."

Caryl tried to pull himself together. "This is important evidence."

The veteran from Salem shook his head. "I thought after the Tassie case the Portland cops got sensitivity training for dealing with the mentally ill."

Tassie was a mentally ill man who died in Police custody.

"What happens now?"

"He'll be tranquilized, maybe admitted, depends on his meds."

Caryl had no comment for that.

"What's your name again, detective?" The title was spoken with derision.

"Caryl Fox. Maybe you can keep me informed of Swenson's progress." He handed over one of his business cards.

The veteran from Salem took it, read it, and put it in his pocket. "You'll be hearing from me." It sounded like a threat. He walked away muttering, "Jesus Christ, don't people have any sense?"

Dazed, upset, and feeling guilty, Caryl returned to the garage where he'd parked the patrol car. He sat for a long time in the front seat, trying to decompress. He remembered the recorded routine when he phoned the VA hospital, "Do you have any thoughts of harming yourself?" He didn't, but Swenson might. What had Swenson said before he collapsed? "That kid." A boy screaming for his father who must be the one Hamilton had killed.

Caryl turned on the overhead light in the patrol car and studied the fatal photograph. A small boy had been watching Hamilton torture and murder the prisoner. Could that part of the photo be enhanced?

That was a long time ago and in Vietnam. The war was over, but some people had long memories and did not forgive. Where was that Vietnamese boy now? Had he grown up in Communist Vietnam or escaped?

The kid's anguished expression had imprinted forever on Vaughn Swenson's mind. He could probably remember the screaming.

Apparently Swenson blamed Hamilton for the whole incident. That the lieutenant had subsequently rescued Swenson and got a medal for his heroic deed was an irony. Swenson loses his feet and the officer gets a medal for bravery. No doubt Swenson got a purple heart to go with the crutches and prosthesis.

Swenson said he didn't know Hamilton was still, had still, been alive. Scratch him off the list of potential but improbable suspects.

Chapter twenty-seven

Caryl had never been present when someone had a seizure. He hadn't been prepared. Luckily it had happened in the VA hospital where help was only a few yards away.

He was still in a daze of preoccupation when he returned to his office. There was a phone message. The crime lab had a match for the fingerprint found on the tape that bound Major Hamilton. It belonged to a Mexican who had been fingerprinted and booked, but never convicted of any crime.

Caryl had failed to write down or remember the names of the two sheet rock workers who had been working in the apartment across the hall from Major Hamilton's. The fingerprint belonged to Pedro Rivas. Now all he had to do was find the man and bring him in.

With any luck, this was the murderer and the case was solved. After that traumatic moment at the VA hospital, Caryl now felt exhilarated. He was ready, if you excuse the expression, for the kill., the gotcha moment he had been hoping for.

Caryl rushed back to the Rose Plaza and back up to the twelfth floor. Someone was still working in the apartment across from Hamilton's, but the door was closed. Caryl knocked and it was opened by a Ukrainian.

Caryl showed his badge. "I'm looking for Pedro Rivas."

The Ukrainian shook his head. "No Rivas."

"He's a plasterer, sheet rock worker."

"Ah. I plumber. Sheet rock all done. Also carpeting."

Of course, the remodel team was made up of specialists who worked from apartment to apartment, each doing their part of the job. "So where's Rivas now?"

The Ukrainian shrugged. "Maybe fifth floor."

It was what Mrs. Seller had explained. As fast as a tenant died, her apartment would be gutted and remodeled to the specifications of the next tenant. There could be three or four apartments in some state of refurbishing at any given time. It was a big building.

Caryl took the freight elevator down to the fifth floor and found the apartment being remodeled, but the door was closed and locked. Frustrated, he continued down to the street level, crossed the breezeway and had to be buzzed in at the entrance. He no longer had Hamilton's keys and fob.

Mrs. Grafton was at her desk nursing the last of her second cup of coffee. "Detective Fox. Have you found the killer yet?"

"I need to contact the sheet rock worker, Rivas."

"The name isn't familiar."

"He's part of the remodel crew working the twelfth floor apartment."

"Then he's not on our payroll. We contract that work out."

"Can you give me the name of the company, who's in charge?"

She looked it up. "It's Chang construction." She wrote the number down on a sticky note.

"Chang?"

"It's a Chinese company," Mrs. Grafton explained. "I believe Mr. Chang invested a chunk of money. Much as I disapprove, the US Government will sell a green card to someone who puts up a lot of money and creates jobs. "

Caryl had heard of the program. It was a scheme rich Chinese used to get some of their wealth out of China and buy some insurance in case the regime clamped down on them with alleged arrests for corruption. He thought of the Mexicans and the Ukrainians. "At least he hires a lot of immigrants."

There must be a pool of new immigrants desperate for jobs and possibly willing to work for less than the minimum wage if they didn't know the law.

Caryl knew from his work in Vice that there was more to slavery in America than just the sex trade. Immigration had busted a restaurant that kept its Chinese workers in virtual confinement while they worked off the cost of their passage to America. Was Chang into that sort of abuse? Or was he on the up and up?

Back in his patrol car Caryl called the number, asked for Mr. Chang.

The woman who answered was coolly efficient. Chang was not available. "He is away on a business trip." Caryl suspected it was a dodge. Chang might well be in his office playing hard to get.

"This is Detective Caryl Fox of the Portland Police. I am trying to locate a Mexican worker on your remodel crew, Pedro Rivas."

The word "police" worked. She was now more cooperative. The receptionist didn't know Rivas. "We have many people working for us, Detective."

"Can you look him up? I need an address. If he's on the job now I need to find him."

She was uncertain. She put him on hold. The music that played while he was waiting was somehow Oriental. Finally she came back on the line. This time she sounded nervous. "I found Pedro Rivas, or I should say I haven't found him. I checked with his foreman. Rivas quit."

"Quit?"

"His foreman says it was a family emergency. He has gone back to Mexico."

"He was working with another Mexican. Can you get me his name?"

She searched again. "You should probably talk to his foreman."

"And that would be?"

"Mr. Phung. Charlie Phung. I can give you his cell phone number."

Caryl called the number and was switched to voice mail. "This is Detective Caryl Fox of the Portland police.. Please call me back. I need to locate one of your crew, Pedro Rivas. "

Rivas was supposed to have left town. How did he travel? By bus? Plane? Did he drive? And where in Mexico was his destination? All Caryl had was a hit on a single fingerprint. Was that enough to put out a bulletin and catch Rivas at the border? Just because the man's fingerprint was on a piece of tape didn't make him a murderer. It didn't necessarily put him at the scene of the crime, either.

How would Chief Bellingham react if Caryl wanted an all points bulletin on the strength of a single finger print??

Caryl was pulling into the precinct garage when his cell phone rang. He thought that was quick. Phung must have got the message.

It wasn't Phung. It was Portland's new police chief. She was obviously steaming mad. "Fox, get to my office right away."

Chapter twenty-eight

While making his way to the chief's office Caryl's mind went through many possible scenarios. Maybe J.J. had struck gold in her side of the investigation. Maybe Bartholomew Walker had called his lawyer and was claiming he was being harassed. Or Pastor Hokanson thought he and J.J. were trying to intimidate him. Nowadays everyone who thought they had a grievance was looking for a reason to sue.

The new Portland police chief was a woman. Some of the force thought her appointment by the mayor was a token, an offering on the altar of equal rights for women. Caryl didn't want any part of that sort of rumor or speculation. He was glad enough to keep as low a profile as he could, being transgender. But he couldn't ignore the fact that Chief Bellingham, being a woman who crashed the glass ceiling, had to be tough. A woman in her job had to be better than a man, tougher than a man.

For Caryl it was enough to be more or less accepted as a man. He was low key. Chief Bellingham was hot button. She also wore a spit and polish uniform like some Pentagon general without the combat ribbons.

Just in case he needed backup, Caryl carried his file on Major Hamilton with him and stood in front of her desk at military at ease position, hands behind his back., hiding the file folder.

Bellingham wasted no time on preliminaries. "What the hell happened at the VA hospital this morning?"

So that was it. "I interviewed a disabled veteran from Salem about the Hamilton murder."

"Interviewed? You put the man in the psych ward."

"I thought he had an epileptic seizure."

"He had a PTSD flashback."

"I didn't have any idea..."

Bellingham took a deep breath to calm down. She shook her head. She motioned to a visitor's chair. "Sit. Tell me your side of this story"

Caryl sat, folder on his lap, and summarized the case along with the murder of Long Nguen, the Asian prostitute. "The death of Major Hamilton has the marks of a ritual murder. It's an ancient and primitive act to eat the victim. In some cultures you might eat the heart of your enemy to gain his courage." Not knowing whether Bellingham was a Catholic or not, he didn't bring up the symbolic Eucharist ritual of the blood and body of Christ.

"So you think that's what happened to Mr. Hamilton?"

Caryl sighed. He thought about Hamilton's son's accusation. "The major's son claims his father was a war criminal."

"Really?"

"The government considered Hamilton to be a hero, gave him a Silver Star medal for rescuing Swenson. When the coroner examined Hamilton's body he found the medal stuffed down the major's throat."

Bellingham nodded thoughtfully. "So you think this was a revenge killing?"

"There was a roll of 35 millimeter negatives in the Major's safety deposit box. I thought prints might reveal something, so I had copies made."

Bellingham had the bill on her desk. "That's where this bill for three hundred and fifty dollars comes from?"

Sheepishly, Caryl admitted it. He indicated the folder on his lap. "I hoped that Swenson might recognize the photos and explain the incident."

"I understand the logic. What did you show him?"

Caryl took out the sequence that showed Lieutenant Hamilton torturing and killing the prisoner. He slid the pictures across the desk to the chief. "Hamilton was just a lieutenant then. Apparently he was hated by his men.

"That seems to have been common in the Vietnam war. "New lieutenant thinks he knows it all and takes charge of war weary grunts who may be doped up."

Bellingham studied the photos. She was obviously sickened. "So that's what triggered Swenson's flashback."

Caryl shook his head. "I don't think so. I think it was the boy there in the corner of the picture. Apparently Hamilton went berserk and ordered his men to wipe out the whole settlement. The boy alerted nearby Viet Kong and in the counter attack Swenson lost his feet to a grenade. It's in the citation for the medal."

"I see."

Caryl explained. "I think it's the face of the boy there that imprinted on Swenson. I didn't notice that when I first saw the prints."

"So Swenson had a flashback and a seizure."

Caryl nodded. "I didn't expect that."

Bellingham returned the photos. "You're a veteran, too, Detective Fox."

"Sort of. I got a medical discharge."

"Then you have access to VA services?"

"Yes."

"I got a complaint about your behavior. I don't think it warrants a reprimand, but I want you to attend a support group for veterans with PTSD as part of your sensitivity training."

'Yes, sir, er Ma'am. Is that all?"

"Next time you have an expenditure like over three hundred bucks for some photographs, I want you to submit it for approval.

Caryl was dismissed. Chastened, he returned to Casey's old office and the suicide desk chair. Tilt too far back and you would be a casualty. Every profession has its hazards.

He phoned J.J. to bring her up to date. "I met with the disabled vet Hamilton rescued. Showed him some photos that triggered a PTSD flashback and seizure. Now I'm in deep shit with the chief."

"Lucky you."

"Have you found out anything about Long's two clients?"

"The bank won't open Hawkin's records. Client confidentially."

Caryl remembered the fine print in the privacy policy the credit card people and banks always sent out. "But police have access."

"Sure, but the Wells Fargo bank wants to see a warrant."

"I suppose we can get Hamilton's son's permission to see his father's statements. He's been cooperative."

J.J. had also checked the license plate reader records, but Hawkins' car was usually garaged. Unless his car and the police roving camera were in the same place at the same time, there was no tracking the vehicle. She did learn that Hawkins drove a Cadillac with On Star service. She would find out if their tracking record put Hawkins' car at Rocky Butte at the approximate time of Long's murder.

J.J. also reported, "I quietly asked the bookkeeper at Hokanson's church if he'd been dipping into the petty cash."

"And?"

"No such record. She isn't always present when they count up the proceeds from the Sunday collection plates. It's possible that Hokanson sets some of that money aside for his so called prayer sessions with Long Nguen. Before the money gets into the record."

"So we don't have proof of embezzlement."

J.J. laughed. "Don't need proof. If he thinks we have it, that's enough. We're not going to charge him with stealing from the church coffers. It's a murder case, Caryl. We just need a confession."

"I think the man's too timid to strangle someone."

J.J. chuckled. "You think so? Since when are you a judge of someone's character? I mean, you didn't anticipate that business at the VA hospital."

"OK, so I don't know if a Lutheran pastor is capable of strangling his hooker. I admit it." He changed the subject. "The fingerprint the crime lab identified as belonging to the Mexican Rivas, but he's skipped. Quit his job. Said he's going to Mexico for a family emergency."

"Emergency like being arrested for cutting Hamilton's throat?"

Caryl didn't know. "Possibly the real perp wanted him out of the way. Maybe Rivas is dead and in the trunk of a car in the Willamette."

J.J. disagreed. "If this was a drug case and the cartel was involved, that might be the case, but this is a simple murder of an old man in a retirement home."

"I don't think there's anything simple about it."

'So where do we go from here?"

Caryl looked at his notes. "I got the name of the Foreman of the remodel crew. Then there's the Vietnamese Orphans outfit. The one that gets the Major's bequest. He had some connection there."

Caryl could almost hear J.J. thinking. "You think Major Hamilton had a guilty conscience about what happened in Vietnam? Might have something to do with his fixation on Asian girls."

"Could be. Mrs. Seller said he was a recluse but I knew he went to a gentlemen's club with naked Asian pole dancers. Then he had Long come to his apartment for sex. So far nobody's seen her come and go. She could have been let in the back exit and sneaked up in the freight elevator. If she killed him, that's how she could have left the building?

"Or his killer could. What about CCT cameras" Did she drive or take a cab? Vehicles would show up."

Caryl admitted, "I haven't got that far yet. You know, it's a big building with lots of come and go traffic. Not everybody signs the register and wears their little guest sticker. The remodel crews are supposed to wear ID badges, but not the guys I've seen. Not Rivas, for sure. They've got the run of the place."

"You think the Major was hiding because he had PTSD or because he was afraid of something?"

"Maybe both. I could imagine he was like the old sea captain in Treasure Island."

"What?"

"Maybe you never read it as a kid."

"I read Trixy Belton mysteries. That's why I wanted to be a cop."

Caryl laughed. He had read those himself when he was a girl. "In Treasure Island the old pirate hides out afraid his bloodthirsty crew will catch up with him for their share of the treasure. One shows up, Blind Pew, and gives him the black spot."

"The black spot?"

"A curse cut out of the cover of a bible. One look and the old pirate drops dead."

J.J.'s voice took on a teasing tone. "OK, Caryl, let's go to the Vietnamese Orphan's Association and see if there's some blind guy carrying a black spot."

"I'll check them out. Someone may have known the Major or Long. We can go to their next meeting. Maybe they give out fortune cookies with a curse inside."

Chapter Twenty-nine

It was not enough for Caryl to look up the Vietnamese Orphans Association in the phone book. Best to do some web surfing first to learn not only the location but the history. He had to admit his ignorance. The Vietnam War was virtually unknown history to him. He was too young to have taken part in peace marches. He had not spit on dazed, depressed, and confused returning veterans and called them baby killers. He had, of course, seen old news clips of the desperate mobs at the gates of the US Embassy in Saigon, now Ho Chi Min City, desperate to get on that last escape helicopter as the city fell to the North Vietnamese Communists.

Caryl's only real exposure to the Vietnamese refugees in Portland was the dry cleaner on Barbur Boulevard. He had no knowledge of Vietnamese culture or history. He had passed Vietnamese restaurants on Sandy Boulevard but never eaten in one of them.

Caryl wasn't one of the Portland foodies who sampled the two hundred food carts on the streets. For him food wasn't an adventure but a necessity. Certainly, he had graduated from burger joints and fast food places that served up grease and salt.. He had gotten as far as Fong's Chinese restaurant and was satisfied. That was where he habitually got his lunches. Having something stable and routine in a chaotic life helped. Egg drop soup and spring rolls were his comfort food. He needed no culinary adventures or challenges.

Living in a Multnomah Village apartment above a bakery meant being satiated with the smell of pastry. Having lived with the fragrances, he didn't have to eat it, too.

Someone else might find him boring, but to tell the truth, his new job was challenging enough, that plus his preoccupation with dealing with his gender as a man.

For him the Vietnamese connection was new. What he did realize almost immediately was that Hamilton's son Arthur might make good use of the Orphans' Association if he was trying to locate his birth mother. Caryl knew that Aaron Hamilton's wife had not had children herself and that Arthur was adopted.

What if the Major was Arthur's actual father? Best to suggest he get a DNA test before the body was cremated and the cremains interred in the National Cemetery. Arthur had told him that his parent's marriage was strained. If the Major had an affair in Vietnam and rescued the baby but not the mother, Mrs. Hamilton might have resented her husband's infidelity and rejected the child.

No wonder Arthur Hamilton was screwed up.

So was the major. Arthur saw him as a war criminal and Caryl had the pictures to prove it. The major had hated the communists but fixated on Asian girls. It looked to Caryl like the Major was haunted by his past deeds, a conflicted man traumatized and fearful, but lustful at the same time.

Had Long taken advantage of the major's weakness to exploit him? Or was he just another john willing to pay a weekly retainer? Did he think she was in love with him? There was no limit to the stupidity of a man with a hard on, or the rage.

Syracuse might not be the best place to search for birth records, but Portland had a large foreign population, many Vietnamese, five thousand Russians, Ukrainians, a long established Chinese and Japanese population. It was an international city. Perhaps that mix helped make Portland tolerant of subcultures, like the gay, lesbian, and transgender community. He would tell Arthur Hamilton about it. Perhaps he'd check it out before he flew back to Syracuse.

If anyone had actually known Arthur's birth mother, this might be a place to look. You never knew. Odd coincidences could happen.

The two murders seemed connected, the Viet vet and the Vietnamese prostitute. Caryl and J.J. drove together in her unmarked to visit the Orphans Association office. She noticed he carried the Hamilton file with him all the time.

"What is that, Caryl? Your security blanket?"

She made him feel sheepish. "I keep hoping I'll find something, some clue, like the picture of the kid who witnessed the murder in Vietnam. Sometimes a solution is in plain sight."

J.J. sighed. "I think you're worried that this is your first really big case and if you blow it they'll send you back to Vice tailing street hookers and busting johns for a misdemeanor fine."

"Don't rub it in. Long's murder is a big one for you, too."

It might not be, except for the connection with Major Hamilton. To the general public reading the Oregonian, the death of another prostitute hardly raised an eyebrow. A story of a lost dog that found its way home across country had more impact. Losing a dog was a story most people could relate to. Death of another whore? Who cared? The case of Major Hamilton and his Vietnamese-American prostitute, both murdered, had captured Caryl and J.J. even if most other people wouldn't care. They had to solve it. It was becoming a matter of honor.

The Vietnamese Orphans had an office in an old store front in the same block as a community center. It was one of those locations that sometimes got rented briefly as a party headquarters before an election, and then reverted to emptiness. The store windows needed cleaning and the posters taped inside the glass were faded. Inside there were several old folding chairs and others that could be set up if there were a committee meeting.

The only person there was an elderly woman who looked tired like she'd been stuck as watch person in the unlikely event that anybody showed up.

J.J., more assertive than Caryl, who tended to be uncertain in unfamiliar circumstances, led the way. "This is Detective Caryl Fox and I'm J.J.."

The old woman's eyebrows rose as if she expected trouble.

Caryl said, "Nothing to worry about. We have some good news. Your Association is to get an inheritance."

"An inheritance?"

"Yes. The Orphans Association is mentioned in the will of Aaron Hamilton who died last week."

"Oh?" She looked like she was searching her memory for a Hamilton.

J.J. explained. "He was a veteran of the war." In this context there was no need to be specific about which war.

The woman frowned. "What is it, blood money?" She seemed bitter.

"I don't think so," J.J. explained. "He adopted a Vietnamese baby. I think he was grateful."

Caryl remembered his thoughts about the birth mother issue. "Maybe Arthur Hamilton should make a formal announcement of the bequest at your next meeting. He is half Vietnamese." He then remembered half Vietnamese might be the wrong thing to say. If the Vietnamese were like the racist Koreans, a mixed race child could be a non-person.

"The next meeting is tomorrow night at the community center next door. Seven-thirty. Everybody welcome."

"Even war veterans?"

She gave him a wise and tired look. "In a war all survivors are veterans."

Caryl agreed. Swenson was a survivor, too, more or less. Currently, thanks to Caryl's blunder, somewhat less.

"Thank you," J.J. said. "We will come. Here is my card."

Caryl hesitated at the door and turned back. He took out the selfie picture of the Major and Long. He folded it so only the girl's face showed. "Do you know this girl?"

She studied it for a moment long enough for Caryl's anticipation to build. Her frown said she knew Long but didn't like her. "She come sometimes. Usually with her sister. Her sister nice girl. Work in restaurant."

"You know Long Nguen was murdered?"

"Everybody know that. In newspaper."

The Oregonian never missed a crime or a sports story.

They left. As they got in J.J.'s unmarked she asked, "Why didn't you show her the major's picture, too?"

"The picture's been in the papers. That lady is an Asian Mrs. Seller. She's a party line to all the gossip."

"You could tell that?"

Caryl almost laughed. "The best observers and informants are old ladies and little kids who have nothing better to do than notice everything. If asked they all see themselves as junior detectives."

J.J. started the car.

Caryl took a chance. "It's almost lunch time. Want to join me? I have a favorite Chinese place. I know you prefer halal food, like Jews who keep kosher, but Jews always like Chinese."

She was reluctant.

"They have a shrimp plate. You eat shrimp?"

She laughed. "OK, but I buy my own food."

"Great." Caryl got out his cell phone. He had programmed in Arthur Hamilton's number. "I want to remind Hamilton to have a DNA check and tell him he should join us for the meeting of the Orphans Association. He should be the one to officially announce his father's bequest."

J.J. gave him an admiring look. "You're a smart guy, Caryl. That sounds to me like a reconciliation."

"Why not?" He hesitated. "And thanks for the guy part." It made him feel accepted.

Chapter Thirty

Assuming that the murder of Major Hamilton might be an inside job, possibly done by Rivas the Mexican plasterer, Caryl hadn't yet followed up on the remaining CCT recordings at the Rose Plaza. Now he returned to them. He had figured out that it was possible to move within the building without being noticed—the freight elevator and the emergency rear exit, as Mrs. Seller had pointed out. Still, one had to get to the building, and there were motion activated outdoor cameras.

Caryl knew that the Tri-Met busses with their nine built-in cameras had the recordings recycled after a week, but he didn't know if that was the case at the Rose Plaza.

He was directed to the IT manager, a busy technical supervisor who still had time for gossip. The IT manager's name tag bore only his first name, Arlan. "We don't dump the old CCT recordings," he explained with pride. There's so much storage on the hard drives, we can keep that stuff forever. Then there's the cloud…"

"I just need the weekend of the Hamilton's murder, say Friday through Sunday."

"What are you looking for?"

"Hamilton had regular Friday visits from a hooker."

The IT manager thought that was funny. "You mean like Meals on Wheels? Sex delivered?"

Caryl didn't laugh. "Or pizza? Why not? This is Portland."

"So what exactly are you looking for?"

"The girl in this picture." He showed the self-portrait taken with Hamilton's phone. "And night time hours. I don't think she visited during the day. I'm especially interested in who shows up at the rear assisted living entrance."

"No problem. I'll get you the recordings from that monitor. You know how to use a computer?"

Feeling insulted, Caryl realized that the IT manager had to deal with a lot of old people who grew up with crank telephones and Ma Bell.

He was set up in a ground floor back office cluttered with shelved electronic equipment in some sort of arrested repair and started searching.

Fortunately, the images were all time stamped. Unfortunately, the clarity was not so great. Caryl scrolled through Friday evening. At nine o'clock a radio cab pulled up by the Rose Plaza rear entrance and a small woman got out, her face hidden by a loose hood. She didn't walk up to the Plaza rear door, but moved out of the field of view of the camera.

Caryl knew where she was going: to that rear emergency exit, accessible only if someone waited inside and held the door open. He scrolled further, and about midnight the radio cab was back. The same person got in and it drove away.

He would contact radio cab and talk to the driver. Where had he picked the girl up, and where did he drop her off later? Caryl was pretty sure he knew.

He didn't stop there. He still had Saturday and Sunday to check. There was a lot of traffic. People were moving in and out. One moving van delivered household goods, another, which arrived later, was from the Salvation Army, picking up what was probably furniture heirs didn't want when granny died. All of those seemed normal, and it created a traffic jam in the driveway.

One truck did not seem normal for a Saturday. It was a white panel truck with the company logo of Chang Construction. The company receptionist had said that Mr. Chang was out of the country, but at the time of the murder he might have been inspecting the work done by his crews on Saturday when they weren't around. That was typical of some sneaky managers. If he showed up while they were at work they might be intimidated and pretend to work harder. Coming in on a Saturday would allow Mr. Chang to inspect at his leisure.

Caryl didn't like that management style. Though he locked the office at the precinct when he wasn't there, the chief would have a pass key. Security of police files was important. Caryl didn't like someone snooping in his drawers unless they had a warrant. It was a betrayal of trust.

On the other hand, it didn't have to be Mr. Chang himself. It could be any one of the crew coming in on an off day to "liberate" company property, like the employee who walks off with power tools.

Some thieves were so brazen that they would walk into a busy office and lift purses hung on the backs of secretaries' chairs. The world was full of thieves.

Caryl paid close attention to the images of the Chang Construction van to see if whoever drove it carried stuff out of the building. All he saw was someone's back. Then it was gone. Just that one stop on Saturday morning. The van had been parked an hour and forty-six minutes.

How many apartments were being remodeled at the same time? Caryl remembered something about three, on various floors of the twelve storey Tower. The way the crews worked, the specialists moved from one apartment to another as the remodel went through various stages like plastering, painting, carpeting, cabinetry, electrical. It was complicated and continuous, like painting the Golden Gate Bridge, never done and then done over.

Maybe he could find out who of Chang Construction had been there that Saturday. In the meantime, he'd contact Radio Cab.

Chapter Thirty-one

Like a gold rush prospector Caryl hit pay dirt when he called the dispatcher at Radio Cab. He learned that it was a cooperative, that the drivers were veterans and co-owners of their cabs. Specifically, the Friday evening visits to the Rose Plaza were under a contract. Every Friday, for at least the last year, the same person was picked up in time for a nine o'clock delivery and then picked up again at midnight. The dispatcher assumed this was a weekly visit from a relative, perhaps a resident's daughter.

When Caryl heard what the address was, he laughed. The passenger had been picked up and delivered at Long's address in Northeast Portland. The rides were charged to Major Hamilton's account. "Not a relative," he explained. "That was Major Hamilton's what you might call his mistress. In fact, he was her Friday client. She had other regular clients for Thursday and Wednesday. I don't know about other days."

A call from a detective about a prostitute made the dispatcher nervous. "Are you with the vice squad?"

"Not any more. This is a murder investigation. The woman who was picked up and delivered on Friday nights was a sex worker. She's been murdered."

The dispatcher wasn't surprised. In a low tone she confided in Caryl. "Radio Cab is not in the sex trade, detective. I admit some motels give kickbacks to drivers who direct johns and their hookers to their businesses. It's just a business referral, like if you ask a driver for a good restaurant. The driver hands over a business card and tells his fare to show the card to the waiter for a discount. That's how drivers made extra money on the side."

"I get it," Caryl said. "But if the john is asking where he can find a girl for the night the driver is technically a procurer. He's pimping." Kickbacks from whore houses were one of the practices he had run into when he worked Vice.

The dispatcher backed off. "I don't know anything about that. Radio Cab is a transportation company. What the drivers do on the side is their own business."

"I'd like to talk to the driver who picked up that fare last Friday. His fare is probably the last person to see Major Hamilton alive."

"That would be Pat, short for Patricia, not Patrick" the dispatcher corrected. "One of our few women drivers." There was a pause while the dispatcher got the message. "You think she could be your murderer?"

"Not mine, I hope." Caryl couldn't imagine Long being strangled with her panties by a female cab driver, but you never knew. "Your driver may be a witness."

"You think Pat's in danger?"

Caryl knew the cab driving was a hazardous business. Robberies were frequent and sometimes deadly. For a woman to drive a cab at night in Portland took some guts. But then, if picking up and delivering Long was a regular contract fare, the risk would be less. Hookers didn't rob drivers. They needed them for referrals. "Not to worry. The passenger I'm talking about is dead."

"Pat usually works nights. She's probably home sleeping. I'll give you her number." She did.

Caryl hung up but before he could connect with the driver he got a call from the crime lab. "You still working that case with J.J? The Asian girl who was strangled?"

"Yes. But I was told there were no fingerprints."

"Did you see the body?"

Caryl sensed he had missed something. "Just the face when we first brought in." Now he could kick himself for just hanging out in the parking lot while J.J. accompanied Mr., Nguen for the identification.

He could hear the "gotcha" tone of the crime lab technician's voice. "So you didn't see she had a couple of broken fingernails."

"No."

"She put up quite a fight for a hundred pound girl. Scratched her killer's face. We're studying DNA scraped from under her fingernails."

Caryl felt excitement rising. He remembered the bandage on Pastor Hokanson's cheek. He'd claimed it was a scratch from a blackberry bush. "How long will that take?"

"Depends. It's not the same as matching a fingerprint in the FBI national files. We're not that advanced when it comes to DNA matching. Of course, if the perp had recently been in the military, the DNA would be on file."

"The military have my DNA, too."

The clerk was surprised. "You a veteran, too? What war?"

"The war between the sexes."

The clerk remembered. Caryl's gender was well known in the department. "Sorry I asked."

"No problem. So now I look for someone who has scratches, probably on his face."

"Or her face."

"I think I know one."

"Check it out. Now all you have to do is bring the killer in. Should be easy."

Caryl caught the irony. So far nothing had been easy. "Thanks a lot." Caryl had heard about 23 and Me, an outfit that told people who sent in their samples what their origins were. The DNA sample you gave could identify what? Racial characteristics? Region of origin?"

The technician was still talking. Maybe he was lonely, working in a lab with nobody to talk to but his microscope. Corpses aren't much for conversation. "DNA will tell us something, but not whether your killer was left handed or had one blue and one brown eye. Mostly we go for a match."

"I'll call J.J. about this. The Fong case is in her neighborhood."

He wondered how she could go about getting Hokanson to give her a DNA swab.

Caryl felt he was making some progress. He phoned J.J. and told her about the crime lab report. "It means we should revisit the pastor and ask for a DNA sample."

"I can do that," J.J. suggested. "What about you?"

"I'm going to check on the cab driver. Turns out it's a woman."

He dialed Pat's number, got an answering machine, and left a message that she call Detective Caryl Fox about one of her fares. To make sure he got a call back Caryl hinted that there might be a $2500 Crime Stopper reward. Cab driving didn't pay that much, and if there was a reward it might be enough to persuade Pat to reveal inside information, like which motels paid a kickback for a by the hour bed rental.

The risk when dealing with informants was if they had no real information they might make something up just to get paid. Wasn't that how some Italian creep got the United States into war with Iraq by forging a letter about yellow cake uranium?

Next: remind Arthur Hamilton to come to the meeting of the Vietnamese Orphans outfit. Make the big speech. Then ask about his birth mother. That shouldn't take much persuasion.

Chapter Thirty-two

Pat did call back. Caryl preferred a face to face interview. He didn't want to drag the driver down to the precinct where the surroundings would be intimidating. Better to meet her on her own turf. She agreed.

She opened the door on the safety chain, not more until Caryl showed his badge. She let him in.

Pat turned out to live in a cluttered studio apartment, not much more than a room with a one butt galley. It was the kind of accommodation previously homeless people, recovering addicts or alcoholics, were housed in to keep them off the street and in safe surroundings. Housing in Portland had become more and more expensive, the prices going up exponentially, which was why Caryl had to settle for a rather shabby one bedroom over a bakery.

Pat hadn't bothered to get dressed for the interview. She was wearing a faded pink bathrobe over pajamas and had not fixed her face or her hair. She was middle aged and didn't look to Caryl like a veteran, but who did?

She didn't resemble the vets he had seen at the VA hospital. They might have pride of service in spite of their poverty. The homeless vets had lost hope. With Pat he detected a measure of defiance, which explained why she hadn't made her bed before he showed up. Or maybe she didn't give a damn.

"Detective Caryl Fox," he said as he came into the room. "You a veteran?" Didn't she have to be to work for Radio Cab, a veterans' company?

Her smile was bitter. "I came in the Marines under don't ask, don't tell. Somebody told." So that was it. She didn't have to explain that she was a dyke.

"Me, too," Caryl said, working on her empathy. "The Army didn't like transgender people, either."

She studied his face and laughed. "We could have got it on, Detective Fox."

Embarrassed, he said, "Not today. I need to know about your fare, the Asian girl you regularly picked up and delivered to the Rose Plaza on Friday nights."

"Miss Nguen. Not my type."

"She was strangled and dumped at Rocky Butte after her picture was published in the Oregonian." He took out the now rather battered selfie. "That's her client, Major Hamilton. He lived at the Rose Plaza. He was murdered not long after her Friday night appointment."

"Oh, shit." Pat sat down on the rumpled bed. "There goes one of my regulars. Not that contract customers do much tipping, but she was safe and steady."

Pat had just gone down a couple of points in Caryl's assessment. She was more concerned about losing a customer than the death of a pretty Asian girl, hooker or not. "So when you picked her up around midnight that Friday, how did she behave?"

Pat shrugged. "I didn't notice. She was tired. Didn't talk much."

"You realize, she might have murdered her client. I'm talking about maybe bloodstains on her clothes, anything like that."

"How did she kill him? Poison? Stabbing?"

"I'm not saying she did kill him. I just have to explore every possibility."

"She was wearing a rain jacket with a hood to hide her face. I didn't see any blood. All she said was she wanted to get home and take a shower."

Caryl nodded. "After sex."

"I guess."

"Was she alone? I'm thinking she might have had an accomplice."

"She was alone."

There was a pause. Caryl broke it with, "Is driving for Radio Cab your only job?"

"I wanted to work in a medical marijuana store, but they got robbed. I decided it was safer to work in day care. Three year olds don't carry guns."

"Agreed."

"And I like kids. Don't have one of my own. Don't have a partner."

"These things get complicated." Having children had never been on his to do list. He had trouble enough just being a man.

Caryl moved to go. "Here's my card in case you need to contact me. I used to work in Vice. My co-worker is J.J. She's still in that department. She could use a tip now and then."

Back in his patrol car, Caryl took notes. What a life, he thought, thinking of Pat. Whatever became of normal? Then again, this was Portland. Weird was normal.

He didn't want to dwell on other people's lives. He had his own to contend with, and of course, there was Arthur Hamilton and whoever killed his father and Long Nguen. Best to stay focused.

Chapter Thirty-three

It didn't take much persuasion to talk Arthur Hamilton into coming along to the meeting of the Vietnamese Orphans' Association. The faint possibility of a lead to his birth mother was enough. Caryl had the major's kill book and the prints from the 35mm film, a couple of which showed the major, then a lieutenant, with a couple of Vietnamese women, probably bar girls.

Caryl had his ever present file folder with him when he picked up Arthur Hamilton at the Rose Plaza. Up to then he hadn't paid much attention to those usual posed pictures of GI's standing by their equipment. He was mainly interested in the ones Arthur saw as proof of war criminality. But there were two other prints. Those showed the then young lieutenant Hamilton showing off with his arms around two pretty Asian girls.

As he turned the patrol car down the ramp that led to the 405 Caryl slipped the two pictures to Arthur who sat beside him. "Could one of these be your mother?"

"No idea."

In his search of the Major's effects, Caryl had not found any letters. They might have helped. Caryl admitted, "It was a long time ago. People change."

Arthur slumped in the passenger's seat, the prints on his lap. He hadn't been listening. He looked discouraged and tired. "The medical examiner released my father's body. He'd prepaid his cremation."

Caryl nodded. "I remember the lawyer said something about that."

"The ashes will be interred this weekend. The VFW does an honor guard, the whole bit."

"So there's no funeral as such?"

Arthur shook his head. "The woman in the Plaza office suggested that some people do a celebration of life."

"So friends can get together for a sermon and a eulogy? Stuff like that?"

Arthur mumbled, "I don't think my father had any friends."

"Mrs. Seller, the Plaza busybody, said he was a recluse."

"Right. I'm not going to put on any phony celebration." He sounded bitter. "There's nothing in my life to celebrate."

"You going to the cemetery for the honor guard? They'll give you a souvenir flag."

"Any flag my father would get probably has blood on it."

"So what will you do for closure?" Closure, that process by which we let go of the past and move on.

"I said goodbye to him years ago. I don't want his goddamn souvenir flag."

Caryl sighed. "Let me know when they do the burial or whatever. I'd like to be there."

"Why? You didn't know him."

A sudden, hard shower slowed the traffic almost to a halt about the thirty-third street Hollywood district exit.

"Just being a cop, Mr. Hamilton. Sometimes a murderer will show up just to say good riddance or maybe to spit on the grave." He would make a point of being there. You never knew.

That killed the conversation until, thanks to the on board GPS, they arrived outside the community center where the meeting was to take place. Caryl parked on the street outside.

J.J. was already there, her unmarked parked in the lot behind the building. They met outside the front door.

Caryl introduced them. "This is Arthur Hamilton, son of the victim. This is detective J.J., my partner in crime." For J.J.: "Arthur is going to announce the bequest from his father's estate."

J.J., not going to miss any possibility, said, "Do you think these people knew there was money coming if the Major was dead? Could be a motive."

"You mean, if the major told Long about the bequest? Pillow talk?"

"Could be," she agreed. "Lots of motives for murder: jealousy, revenge, money, blackmail, extortion. "

Arthur Hamilton turned up his collar against the rain. "I don't envy you people's jobs. Let's get inside."

J.J. asked, "When are you going back to Syracuse?"

"As soon as possible. Portland's too weird for me."

J.J. joked. "You've been watching Grimm on television. Most of us aren't like that."

Caryl detected a shudder and laughed. Grimm was one of the few television shows he watched, along with Portlandia.

The community center had a riser at the end where performers could stand and be seen. A battered podium was off to one side and a pull down movie screen was at the back wall. Caryl's overall impression of the place was that it was shabby, probably used by a lot of organizations from time to time, but not kept up. It had obviously not been painted in years. Northeast Portland was the home of many ethnic groups and the community center showed it. On one wall hung a faded map of Vietnam showing a demarcation line. The name of the capitol was Saigon. Had it been a new map it would be Ho Chi Min City. Of course, if this was an organization of refugees and their children, they might be stuck in the past, living on old memories, or like Cuban exiles in Miami who rejected current reality,

Another map, presumably put up by Russian expatriates, was of USSR, Russia and the old Soviet Union. That one showed Leningrad, not St. Petersburg. Portland had about five thousand Russian speaking immigrants. Was that nostalgia for the past, or weren't there any current maps available?

Near the entrance was a welcome table with the same woman they recognized from their visit to the office next door. She surprised Caryl by remembering his name. "Detective Fox." Of course, he had given her his business card. This was one of those see all-know all elderly ladies who pay attention. "Please sign the visitor's book." She indicated a pad and a ball point with a string attached so it would not walk away.

The sign-in sheet included a place for email addresses. Caryl and J.J. signed in with theirs, but Arthur Hamilton did not include an email address. Didn't he have one, or was he avoiding spam? Once someone got your email address you'd be hounded for donations.

Caryl saw Arthur's omission as a mistake. If he wanted help in finding his birth mother, there might be a source in the Orphan's Organization who contacted him later.

They were also expected to write their names on labels and wear them. J.J. wrote hers, Caryl just used his first name, and Arthur did the same. They were no longer anonymous.

There were already a couple of dozen people in the community center, most of them standing around and visiting, but Caryl and J.J. were approached right away by a Vietnamese man about fifty years old. He didn't have a name tag, but introduced himself as Mr. Trung. He was wearing a dark green sports jacket with a foreign cut, narrow lapels. When he shook hands with Caryl his skin was rough and dry, a sign of hard, manual work. He smiled with his mouth, not his eyes which were, if anything, suspicious of strangers. He avoided eye contact with J.J. Presumably they did not have that many Moslem or Caucasian visitors.

"I'm Caryl Fox and this is my associate J.J. This is Arthur Hamilton whose mother was Vietnamese."

"Oh." That simple statement could mean a lot of things, depending on how you wanted to interpret it. It might be followed up with "Was your father an

American? An American soldier? French? Or what?" but Mr. Trung was too polite.

J.J. asked, "What's on the program tonight? Music? Vietnamese dance?"

Mr. Trung shook his head. "We have a video from one of our members who just came back from Vietnam and toured the new factories there."

Arthur Hamilton raised his eyebrows. "Sounds like a lot of changes from when my father was there."

"Was your father in the military?"

Arthur didn't want to talk about that. "My father adopted me after the war. I'm here for a couple of reasons. One is to possibly find out about my birth mother."

"You should talk to someone else. Tracing the parents of orphans of war can be difficult. I'll introduce you."

"I also have an announcement if you'll put me on your agenda. My father left part of his estate to your organization."

"Oh, you are that Hamilton! I didn't make the connection at once."

"Then you have heard about it?"

Mr. Trung was non-committal. "There was a rumor. Talk."

J.J. broke in. "We'd also like to talk to anyone who knew Miss Long Nguen."

The friendly smile disappeared. "The sex worker who was murdered. Yes, we know about that."

"It was in the newspaper," Caryl suggested, thinking that might be an explanation.

"This is a small community. We have many Vietnamese here, but not that many families. People talk."

J.J. got it. "Then you probably know that Caryl Fox and I are both with the Portland police investigating her murder."

"I'm sure anyone who can help will do so."

It didn't sound to Caryl that they would. It was the difference between anyone and someone. 'Anyone who can help' could mean that it was unlikely, but then, not everyone knew the difference between any and some, especially non-native speakers.

Arthur seemed to be uncomfortable with so many strangers. Perhaps he shared his father's tendency to avoid people. Certainly he could not have PTSD from a wartime situation where anyone could be the enemy. Caryl figured that Arthur Hamilton simply didn't have the social skills of people who jumped in anywhere with enthusiasm. Caryl took over. "Who is your expert on family history?"

"That would be Charlie Phung. He has made a study of genealogy. He is over there." Trung gestured toward the stage where a couple of men were in a serious discussion. "I'll introduce you."

He led Arthur through the crowd, with J.J., Caryl following to observe all the action.

Trung waited to interrupt until he caught the eye of one of the two men, a short, stocky man in his fifties, his hair turning grey. "Charlie, we have a visitor interested in family genealogy."

Charlie Phung turned to look at Arthur with bland curiosity. He was not a good looking man. He had a face that recorded a life of troubles. Traumas had left their footprint on his features, lines around his eyes and a perpetual frown to his mouth. He was not a man who smiled very much.

"Mr. Arthur Hamilton," Trung said.

At the mention of Arthur's name Phung's face blanched. He tentatively offered his hand.

Arthur took it like a salesman or a politician who sizes someone up by their grip. Hamilton was not one of those macho men who like to crush your hand, but he had a firm handshake that lingered a shade too long as if touch could plug you into someone's character.

Phung hastily pulled his hand back. "Hamilton?"

"Yes. My father was a veteran who adopted me from a Vietnamese woman. I'm hoping to locate her."

J.J. and Caryl both read Phung's expression, his surprise, and his hesitancy. J.J. saw the moment ripe and introduced herself. "I'm J.J. and this is Caryl Fox. We thought we might assist Mr. Hamilton."

Charlie Phung seemed momentarily reassured. "Do you know Vietnamese family history?"

"Actually not," Caryl said. "We're with the Portland police. We're investigating the murder of Long Nguen."

Charlie Phung pretended not to understand. "What does that have to do with Mr. Hamilton here?"

Caryl was ready to whip out the photograph of the Major and his mistress, but restrained himself. "The girl's death seems to be connected with Mr. Hamilton's father."

Charlie Phung looked down at the floor. "I don't understand."

Arthur explained. "My father put your organization in his will. I think he had bad feelings about the unfortunate war."

Mr. Trung took on the role of mediator. "We all have bad memories, but we try to put them behind us and more on."

"I'm trying to do that," Arthur Hamilton offered.

That surprised Caryl. It was a change of heart. Maybe Hamilton was getting over his anger and his hatred. Like the sign at Pastor Hokanson's church said, Hate the sin, love the sinner. As for Hokanson and sin, well, he may have got his priorities mixed up. Caryl guessed that though Arthur Hamilton was revulsed by the photos of the atrocity in Vietnam, he saw something good in his father's actions afterward.

"Not everyone can," Phung said, apparently trying to be diplomatic. "Some things cannot be forgiven."

J.J. understood. "You mean like the Old Testament says, the sins of the fathers descend upon the offspring until the seventh generation."

Caryl did not know J.J. very well, but he saw that J.J. rejected Old Testament vengeance and collective guilt. He knew from past experience that she tended to be conciliatory, arguing with the Prosecuting Attorney that some sentences would be unnecessarily harsh. The jails were already overloaded. There needed to be mercy for those who made a life altering mistake. She tended to take the side of the sex workers and go after the johns and pimps who exploited them.

Charlie Phung agreed. "There must be justice."

Arthur didn't get it. "I was adopted. I need to find my birth mother if she is alive. How can I find out about adoptions?"

Phung was relieved to get to a topic what was non-threatening. "Do you have a birth certificate, adoption papers?"

"There was something in my father's safety deposit box, but it was in a foreign language I couldn't read."

"If you bring it to me at the office perhaps we can translate it. We can go from there."

"Your office? I'm leaving Portland in a couple of days."

Charlie Phung took his wallet from his hip pocket and extracted a rather beat up business card. "You will find me here." He handed it over.

Arthur Hamilton took it and read aloud, "Chang Construction."

Caryl and J.J. didn't have to wait for Phung's explanation. "We remodel apartments, condos, and so on."

J.J. and Caryl exchanged knowing looks. This could be their guy.

Chapter Thirty-four

As it turned out, Mr. Phung was the president of the association and led the meeting. Once he got everyone's attention and people took seats on the battered wooden folding chairs, he introduced Arthur Hamilton. The audience was unfamiliar to Hamilton. He was reluctant to mount the stage and stand by the podium, but this was his chance and he had to do it.

Taking the hand microphone which he was coached to hold close to his mouth like an ice cream cone, he began. "My father was a veteran who served in Vietnam. When the war ended he rescued me as an orphan and adopted me. I, ah, don't know if he was in love with my birth mother, or if he even knew her. I guess I'm like the baby Moses who was set adrift. But, well, you can see I am bi-racial. I'm obviously the child of a Caucasian, probably an American soldier. I think DNA may prove that my father was my biological father, not just an adopted stranger. I guess if he was my real father it would be easier to adopt me officially even if his name isn't on my birth certificate. But I don't know who my mother is."

At this Arthur Hamilton choked up. "My father is dead, so my only family will be my Vietnamese mother. I hope someone here can help me find her."

Arthur Hamilton paused to collect himself, then remembered. "My father hated the communists, but he loved the Vietnamese people. That's why he included the Orphans Association in his will."

J.J. stood close to Caryl and whispered, "I guess these folks have to decide which is more important, the money or their prejudice against mixed race bastards."

Caryl didn't like that word. "Take it easy, J.J. In the Portland police you and I are both outcasts."

She took his arm and squeezed it. "We got to stick together, Detective Fox."

Caryl was surprised. Normally J.J. avoided being touched. A handshake was as intimate as it got. She was not one of those touchie-feelie people who throw their arms around your shoulder without provocation.

Arthur stepped down from the stage and was immediately approached by a couple of people.

"I think his birth mother is going to turn up," J.J. said.

"It would be a miracle if she were actually in Portland and not dead back in Vietnam."

"I'm glad he didn't go into the nature of his father's death or describe the murder scene."

"Right. That's privileged information the public doesn't need to know."

They retreated to the back of the hall. The ladies of the Association had set out small buns and tea. While they sipped from recyclable paper cups J.J. whispered, "I didn't tell you, but I saw a Chang Construction van parked in the lot."

Caryl remembered the CCT tapes showing the company van parked at the rear entrance to the Rose Plaza on Saturday morning. He already knew that Charlie Phung was the foreman of the remodel crew. Phung had not responded to his voice mail. He hadn't thought to check the CCT tapes of the elevators that had surveillance cameras. Hoping to see the perp coming and going through the entrance Mrs. Seller had suggested, he had focused on the back door to the Plaza. As foreman for Chang Construction Phung probably didn't sign in as a visitor, but came and went without being noticed, an invisible man. If Phung had inspected the several apartments being remodeled, he probably used the common elevators. The recordings were time stamped. He should be able to retrace Phung's movements through the building by comparing the elevator tapes. The more thorough he was, the more likely he could break down Phung's alibi if he were Major Hamilton's killer.

The trouble was, there was no evidence at the scene of the murder other than plaster dust everyone had tracked in from the mess in the hallway. The fingerprint of the Mexican Rivas was flimsy at best and he was gone. Just being in the Rose Plaza at the time of the murder was not evidence. Over five hundred people lived or worked there.

Even if Charlie Phung could be placed at the scene of the crime, that wasn't enough to take to the prosecuting attorney. They needed enough for the prosecutor to take to a grand jury and get a true bill. Only then would there be a trial.

Caryl and J.J. both knew that of crimes committed, only a fraction led to an arrest. Only a small percentage of those went to actual trial, and an even smaller percentage ended in jail time. There was little risk for most criminals. Consider Tyrone Brown, caught at the border trying to smuggle a fourteen year old white girl into the Canadian sex trade. He already had a jail record, but might wriggle a short sentence and community service, claiming he was only helping a runaway girl leave the country. He could say she was a hitchhiker and he had only given her a ride. So go prove it.

Caryl and J.J. had other suspects and the two murders might not be connected at all. If the DNA of Pastor Hokanson matched what was under Long's fingernails, that would be a break, but was it enough? He could claim his Wednesday night "prayer" sessions included rough sex. Maybe they had tussled. The Major had been handcuffed. That could be Long's equipment for S&M sex. If there was reasonable doubt, there might be no conviction of anyone.

Of course, a confession and a guilty plea would solve their problems. No expensive, protracted trial.

It would take considerable interrogations skills to get a confession in the murders of Major Hamilton and Long Nguen. The public were used to seeing body camera and cell phone footage of crimes taking place. The public and the news media were spoiled. The real risks could be lawsuits for false arrest, claims of racism. If a prosecutor falsified evidence there could be censure or disbarment. Desperate Lawyers looking for consignment cases that would produce a big chunk of a settlement were always looking for an opportunity. For Caryl the job wasn't only about solving a crime. It was also about not making an expensive, humiliating, career busting mistake.

Chapter Thirty-five

Standing aft the back of the room and only paying scant attention to the video of the trip to Vietnam's factories, Caryl and J.J. discussed their next move.

"Did you see his body language," Caryl asked. "When the name Hamilton came up? And we identified ourselves as Portland police? The guy looks guilty as hell."

J.J. agreed. "I got the same impression. He's hiding something. So what do we do?"

"Since Charlie Phung is the local family history buff and the boss of Rivas, the Mexican whose fingerprint we have, we can use that lead as an excuse to bring him in. We'll be asking for his advice. He can't refuse to help."

J.J. smiled. It was amazing how pretty she was, in spite of wearing that head scarf that hid her hair. Caryl wondered how she would look without it. "Then we can gradually shift the discussion to whether he ever met Major Hamilton. I'll bet if he's lying I'll catch it."

"Unless he's a sociopath who lies all the time."

Caryl disagreed. "The man is not that smart."

"Could be an act."

"I think he's straight forward. He'll be evasive, but not make up lies."

J.J. took a bite of one of the little buns they'd been offered. "My kindergarten teacher used to say "O what an ugly web we weave when first we practice to deceive.""

"When the movie is over I'll ask him to come in to the precinct for an interview about Rivas. That'll be non-threatening."

"What about Arthur Hamilton?"

"I don't want Arthur Hamilton in the same room with Charlie Phung. It'll put Phung on his guard. I'll offer Mr. Phung coffee and a chat."

J.J. smiled. "Don't forget a donut. Everybody thinks all cops eat donuts. He'll think you're inviting him into the inner circle."

"I need you to be there."

"Why? The Hamilton murder is your case."

Caryl disagreed. "Didn't you catch the hostility to Long Nguen? The old lady in the office made it clear to me that Long's sister Lotus was all right, but not Long. I think the whole Vietnamese community knew she was a hooker. I think she told her sister about the promised bequest and the word got out. Didn't you notice? Everybody knew about it before Arthur made the announcement. No one was surprised."

"So the money is tainted. We Moslems have a tradition. It's called call it blood money."

"Right." Caryl remembered blood money was an alternative. Instead of an eye for an eye, the perp could buy forgiveness with cattle or cash. "It's another issue we can explore when we interrogate Charlie Phung.

"You want me to play bad cop?"

"Not yet. Maybe later. Let's see what he says."

The film was over. Arthur Hamilton was conferring with Charlie Phung and Caryl approached them. "Mr. Phung?"

Charlie Phung was suspicious. "Yes, Detective."

Careful not to show the other photos, the ones from the 35mm roll of film, Caryl took out the photo of Hamilton and Long that had been in the newspaper. "I'm sure you saw this in the newspaper in connection with the murder of Major Hamilton."

Now Phung was on the defensive. "We all saw that. It was in the Oregonian."

"I shouldn't be telling you this. Mr. Phung, but we found a fingerprint at the scene of the murder." Saying that, Cary watched Phung closely. Would he think it was his own? The flicker of fear on his face said yes. Caryl quickly added, "It belonged to one of your workers, Pedro Rivas."

Phung was obviously relieved. "He went back to Mexico."

Caryl feigned a sigh. "I'd very much appreciate it if you could help us find him. He's what we call a person of interest." Caryl gestured around the crowded community center. "This isn't the place for a discussion. Could you come to the First Precinct tomorrow morning, say ten o'clock? We would like to know more about Rivas. Where he lived here in Portland, what friends might give us information about his family in Mexico. You could be a great help."

"I can do that. Ten o'clock?"

Cary gave Mr. Phung his business card. "I'd appreciate it. And afterwards you might meet with Arthur Hamilton and go over the Vietnamese documents he found among his father's effects. You could do him a great service."

Caryl didn't want Charlie Phung alone in that Plaza apartment with Arthur Hamilton. They could meet somewhere public in the building like the cafe or restaurant. If Phung was the killer, it could put Arthur Hamilton in danger. Caryl didn't want risk Arthur as bait.

Caryl slipped the selfie photo back in his file folder. He had plans for the other photos for later.

Chapter Thirty-six

Since Hamilton didn't know Portland, Caryl had offered him a ride to the Vietnamese Orphan's meeting. He didn't know if Arthur had a city map or GPS in the Major's car, so his excuse was he didn't want Arthur to get lost looking for the Orphan's Association meeting. He also wanted some private face time with the younger Hamilton and to warn him. Now, on the way back to the Rose Plaza, he started with, "I think Mr. Phung may be able to help you locate our birth mother if she is alive, but I want you to be cautious."

"What do you mean?"

"Don't mention your claim that your father was a war criminal. Don't mention the war at all. That could put him off, raise old hostilities. He can back out of helping you any time."

Arthur was not as naïve as Caryl hoped. "There's something you're not telling me."

"Charlie Phung is the foreman of the remodel crew next door to your father's apartment."

"Are you saying Charlie Phung is a suspect in my father's murder?"

"I never said that. If I did, it would change the way you behaved around him. I just want you to concentrate on your problem of finding your birth mother."

"I get it."

"Don't invite him to your father's apartment."

"I couldn't. I've been cleaning the place out. There's only one chair left and the bed."

"Good. See him in a public space."

"Uh huh."

They were crossing the Burnside bridge and turning back to the Naito parkway, the quickest way to get to the Rose Plaza.

But Arthur Hamilton was now already suspicious. He sat silently, obviously worried.

Caryl tried to reassure him. "If Mr. Phung backs out on you, I'm sure there are other alternatives. Remember that old Vietnamese lady who was at the welcome table, where you signed the guest book?"

"Yes."

"She's also the person who sits at the association office. She knows everything. If Charlie Phung gets cold feet, I'll bet she's as good a source."

Arthur Hamilton was doubtful. "Well..."

"Relax, Arthur. I'm going to see Charlie Phung at the precinct tomorrow. This is all preliminary. With luck you'll find out that your birth mother is still alive, that she wants to see you, and, if it's a miracle, that she even lives in Portland, which is highly unlikely."

"She might not want anything to do with me." Hamilton sounded glum.

"Don't anticipate the worst. Most of what we worry about never happens."

They pulled up in the breezeway at the Rose Plaza. As Hamilton got out of the squad car, Caryl asked, "Has the medical examiner released your father's body?"

"I don't know."

"And he's being cremated?"

"That's what his plan was."

"And the cremains are going to the National Cemetery here in town?"

"Right."

"But you aren't planning to be there for the honor guard. You said you'd be leaving town as soon as possible."

"Right."

Caryl turned to him. "Don't leave town without calling me first. If you don't mind, I'll go to the cemetery for you. An old warrior needs someone there for the send off. They play taps, you know Three gun salute. The whole bit."

"That's decent of you." Arthur shut the car door.

As he pulled away, Caryl thought, 'not that decent.' He suspected that the murderer would show up to pretend to mourn but in reality to gloat.

Aaron Hamilton's funeral wasn't the only one. There'd be something for Long Nguen, too. He'd have to ask her sister. Mr. Nguen was staying with here. Caryl didn't know how the Vietnamese community would deal with the funeral for a sex worker. Would her mother fly in from Texas? In the olden days, a sinner could not be buried in the church yard's hallowed ground. Her funeral might be shunned entirely. Just as the Major's killer might show up at the National Cemetery, Long's might be among her mourners.

Was Long a Catholic? Buddhist? Or nothing at all? It would be ironic if Long's funeral would be conducted by Pastor Hokanson, a Minnesota Lutheran. How would he phrase a eulogy for a sex worker he patronized? Might be worth showing up just to find out.

When he transferred from Vice to Homicide, Caryl hadn't anticipated going to the funerals of victims. For a second he wondered what he would wear, then laughed at himself for thinking like a woman again. Old habits.

What Caryl needed now was to decompress back in his apartment with a nice cold beer. He had made the appointment with Charlie Phung for ten o'clock. Maybe that was too early. He wanted to retrace Phung's movements on the Saturday of the murder, which meant going over all those elevator surveillance tapes. The IT guy at the Rose Plaza might not be happy about having to set up the system for replay...

Chapter Thirty-seven

He wasn't. Arlan was typical of technicians for whom everything is intuitive.. The IT guy was busy working on the intricate fire warning system and resented the intrusion on his concentration. "My assistant can give you the key. You already know how to work the system." As if one session would have made Caryl an expert.

He was shown to the now familiar room and left to his own devices. It wasn't easy and he had little time before he had to rush off to the precinct for his ten o'clock meeting with J.J. and Charlie Phung.

Still, he was sure of the time frame. The medical examiner had estimated the time of the murder as early Saturday morning. What Caryl needed were enough hits to establish a time line. The Major's apartment was not in view of a CCT camera, but the main bank of elevators was and he could track Charlie Phung's movements in other locations. If he didn't have all the details, he could bluff.

Hastily gathering his notes, he shut down the Plaza system and phoned J.J. to remind her of their meeting at the precinct. Chang Construction was remodeling three Rose Plaza apartments at the same time, but not in the same order of work. Besides the twelfth floor job, the other two were on lower floors and at the north end of the four block long building. The sheet rock stage was early in the sequence, after the apartments were gutted, which meant that the two Mexicans might no longer be needed at the Rose Plaza. Of course Pedro Rivas was allegedly out of the country, if that was true. Chang Construction must have other jobs around Portland. Charlie Phung was a busy man.

Instead of setting up their questioning of Mr. Phung in an interrogation room, Caryl decided to make it in his office as less formal. He covered his white board with all those photos of the crime scene and of the two murder victims, hiding them behind a large white cloth. He had to commandeer another visitor's chair for J.J As she suggested, he remembered to bring along several filled donuts from his landlord's bakery downstairs. They were similar to the buns they'd been served at the Orphans' Association meeting. Caryl wanted Mr. Phung to feel relaxed.

He was, even though the inside of the First Precinct with its bulletproof window at the reception desk could be off putting. If you were a criminal, this was the lion's den.

Caryl was waiting for him inside the entrance and extended his hand in a warm greeting. "So glad you could come, Mr. Phung. Do you mind if I call you Charlie? I'm Caryl."

Phung didn't mind. He sat down in the visitor's chair with his hands clasped in his lap, defensive body language like someone in a dentist's chair. J.J. and Caryl were both behind the desk. "Coffee?"

"Please."

"Cream and sugar? Decaf?"

"Just decaf," Phung said and J.J., at Caryl's nod,. went to fetch some.

 Phung accepted a recyclable paper cup. Styrofoam cups had long since been taboo, part of Portland's green revolution.

"Donut?"

"No thanks."

Caryl apologized. "I'm terrible at taking notes. J.J. here says I am not to make her my secretary, so if you don't mind I'd like to record this conversation. Is that all right, er, Charlie?"

"I suppose so, Detective."

So much for his attempt at cozy informality. "Caryl. Please."

"Caryl."

Caryl turned on the recorder and began, saying "This is Caryl Fox speaking with Mr. Charlie Phung about one of Chang Construction's Mexican workers, Pedro Rivas. Charlie, when did Rivas leave?"

"Last Saturday morning."

"Did he quit or was he fired?"

"He said it was a family emergency."

"So you let him go without notice?"

"I had no choice. His partner phoned the company. Pedro was already gone."

"Did you think he was running away, or something?"

"I don't know. Why would he run away?"

Caryl gave J.J. a sideways glance and reached into his crime scene file but didn't show it yet. "The twelfth floor apartment across the hall from where Rivas was working is the scene of a murder. Did you know that?".

"I saw the crime scene tape. I didn't know what it was for."

"It was the apartment of Major Hamilton. He was murdered."

Charlie Phung didn't react.

Much to Caryl's irritation, J.J, broke in. "Aaron Hamilton was Arthur Hamilton's father. Did you know that?

"No." This time he did react. His frown suggested all hope of helping Arthur in his quest for his mother might be for nothing.

Caryl tried to steer the discussion back to the Mexican worker. "Pedro Rivas's fingerprint was found in the Major's apartment."

"Ah, so you think Pedro killed Mr. Hamilton?"

"We have to pursue all possible leads, Charlie. It's not been made public information, but this is what the crime scene looked like." He took out the photo of the Major taped to the chair, handcuffed, his chest cut open and throat cut, all in digital color.

Phung didn't flinch. He was indifferent. Did that mean he was good at hiding his reactions, that he had seen it all before, or that he wasn't surprised?

"Were you ever in Major Hamilton's apartment?"

"I had no reason to be."

Caryl was aware of the evasive answer, but continued. "Had you ever met Major Hamilton?"

"I think I saw him once in the hallway. We didn't speak."

"How did he react when he saw you?"

"I don't think he liked to talk to people."

"You mean people in general or just Vietnamese?"

Charlie Phung shook his head. "How would I know? I never saw him before."

There was a pause.

J.J. broke in again. "Did you know that Major Hamilton had been in Vietnam? That he was a war criminal?"

Charlie Phung had sipped his coffee. Now he put the cup down on the desk. "I do not think this is about Pedro Rivas."

The carefully engineered atmosphere of cordiality was broken. Now Phung took the initiative. "What does Pedro Rivas have to do with this? Or is this about the war? That was a long time ago. Are you two detectives prejudiced against Vietnamese people?" Now he was playing the race card.

J.J. spoke up defensively. "We are only asking about how Pedro's fingerprint got on the tape used to bind the victim." She pointed to the picture on the table.

"I know nothing about that."

"Is that the sort of tape used by Chang Construction?"

"We use all kinds of tape, masking, duct, insulation." Charlie Phung stood up, pushed the coffee cup away. "I do not like your line of questions. I think if we talk again, I will bring my lawyer."

Caryl tried to reassure him. "You have not been arrested Charlie. This is just a friendly conversation."

"I am not your friend, detective."

Caryl desperately tried to save the situation. If Mr. Phung wanted to see his lawyer that would put everything on a different footing. Caryl wasn't ready for that. "Please. Charlie, don't rush off. J.J. here is investigating the murder of Long Nguen." He showed the picture of her and the Major. "Did you know her?"

"Yes. She sometimes came to the Orphan's Association meetings." His tone indicated that he disapproved.

"Do the members of the Association know she was a sex worker?"

Charlie Phung nodded.

"What do the others thank about that?"

Charlie's face hung down in shame. "She dishonored the community."

J.J. had a thought. "I think her relationship with the Major is connected with his bequest. We think he was in love with her."

Phung shook his head. "I know nothing of that."

"Was she shunned?"

"Shunned?" Phung didn't know the word.

"She means ostracized," Caryl explained.

Phung didn't know that word, either, but he got the drift. "She dishonored all of us."

That word got to J.J. "In some Muslim communities there are honor killings. Does that happen among Vietnamese?"

"Not Vietnamese. If we were Japanese there is a tradition of hari kari if one is dishonored and loses face. We are not Japanese. We are also not Muslims. Most of us are Buddhist, and some Catholic.

To Caryl, who if anything was an agnostic, those cultures were a mystery. "Do you think a Vietnamese would have killed Long Nguen?"

When they first met Charlie Phung at the Orphan's Association and announced they were from the police he was surprised and reacted. Now he was on his guard and stone faced. "I know nothing about it." He stood up. "Now, I must go I have work to do."

They couldn't stop him and he left.

When the two detectives were alone, J.J. apologized. "I blew it."

Caryl would agree, but didn't say so. "Let him bring his lawyer. The more he stonewalls, the more we know he's the perp."

"He didn't even flinch when he saw the photo of Major Hamilton.."

"All the more reason. We have to look into the background of Charlie Phung, do our homework. Maybe he has a rap sheet. Maybe he's in he country illegally. "

J.J. agreed. "Maybe he has an unpaid parking ticket."

Caryl laughed. "That's what I like about you, J.J. You have a great sense of humor. Even the Portland police don't send somebody up for life over a parking ticket."

"Do you think he'll still help Arthur Hamilton find his mother?

"Maybe not. I think I'd better warn him." Caryl' phone was programmed for Hamilton's number at the Plaza. There was no answer.

Caryl put the phone back in his pocket. "Let's not let these donuts go to waste. This time I'll get the coffee. Decaf?"

"No. Regular. After that fiasco, I need a boost."

Chapter Thirty-eight

In spite of their suspicions, they had nothing concrete on Charlie Phung. Of course, as foreman for Chang Construction he had access to the Rose Plaza, but there were almost three hundred and fifty residents and a hundred and eighty employees, so potentially more than five hundred people had access to the twelfth floor. Access was not enough. Access could translate as opportunity, but what about motive?

Pastor Hokanson might had a motive if Long threatened to expose his misuse of church funds to pay for sex. J.J. drove back across the Willamette to get Pastor Hokanson to give her a DNA swab. Hokanson was still a potential suspect. Was that scratch on his face really from a blackberry bush? Would it match DNA from under Long's fingernails?

If Hokanson was the Wednesday client and she scratched him then, surely she would have cleaned her fingernails before the next Monday. Had he seen her later? Broken their regular Wednesday "counseling" routine?

Was it worth checking the debris in Hokanson's back yard to see if some blackberry branch had his DNA on one of those pesky thorns? At what point did being a good detective border on the ridiculous?

She'd got a warrant to look into the financial records of Bartholomew Hawkins. He might have motive, too. She was looking for possible blackmail withdrawals that matched deposits on Long Nguen's accounts. So far, nothing, but it took time.

The more you looked, the wider the pool of potential suspects grew. If you were suspicious enough, everyone was a potential killer.

The murder of Aaron Hamilton wasn't the only killing in Portland. There was a shoot out outside the Perky Nipple gentleman's club on Foster Road, and a man found shot dead inside a coin dealer's store over in Vancouver. There were witnesses to the shoot-out, but the coin dealer killing was probably a robbery. There might be fingerprints and the bullets traceable to a specific firearm. New technology could match casings to a specific firing pin. That was for the technicians to figure out.

The Hamilton murder was, because of its unusual ritualistic nature, more interesting. Were they dealing with a sociopath, a mad man? Many murders were spur of the moment situations, sudden anger, an argument escalating and no planned attempt to cover up. As retired Detective Casey had once told Caryl, most criminals were as dumb as a trout, which was a pretty valid description unless you were a trout fisherman.

Major Hamilton's killer had left no clues except the fingerprint on the tape. Of course, Charlie Phung might have taken the tape from the work site, but was this enough evidence to take to a grand jury? The door to the apartment under construction was not locked. Anybody, like that snoopy Mrs. Seller with her curiosity, could have gone in, not that an old lady would have cut the Major's throat. And who were the next remodel crew? What came after sheet rock? Painting? Plumbing? Electrical? J.J. didn't know. Caryl hadn't talked to any other workers.

Caryl finally got a reply from Arthur Hamilton on his cell phone. "This is Detective Fox again. J.J. and I had a talk with Charlie Phung, your Vietnamese source for all things ancestral. I'm afraid we put him off."

"What do you mean, put him off?"

"He thinks we see him as a suspect."

"Well, you do, don't you?"

Caryl wasn't going to admit that. "He's become a hostile witness. Since you are Major Hamilton's son, which he now knows, he may not want to talk to you about your birth mother."

"Shit."

"Did you arrange to see him, to show him those papers in Vietnamese?"

"Yes."

"When?"

"This afternoon, at the Rose Plaza."

That almost gave Caryl a dry mouth. "Not in your apartment, I hope?"

"No. In the little café on the second floor."

"What time?"

"Two-thirty. He has an inspection to do. Someone else died."

"Not another murder, I hope."

Arthur Hamilton almost laughed. "Come on, Caryl, the average age in that place is eighty-six. Someone dies there every month. Then the next tenant wants the apartment. Busy place."

It looked like the workers for Chang Construction had lifetime employment, like the painters of the Golden Gate Bridge: finish one end and start over. Caryl paused. "Right. Listen, when you talk to Charlie Phung, don't mention the war or war crimes or anything like that. Stick to the birth certificate and adoption papers. Solving your father's murder is not your job. That's ours. Don't try to play detective."

"OK."

"If anything you might mention that you were not on speaking terms with your father. If the war comes up, I mean, if Phung brings it into the conversation, stick to your horror of the war as having been a terrible mistake. Your father had a thing for Asian women. Just don't make it sound like a perversion. You don't know who your mother was, or if she was your father's girl friend, but you could say you think your father loved her and was heartbroken that he had to leave her behind. You need Charlie Phung's support, not his enmity."

"I understand."

Caryl didn't want Arthur Hamilton in danger if Charlie Phung got angry at him. If Phung were the killer, if Phung thought killing the Major was not enough, he might go after the son, too. You could never be sure of how a mentally deranged person would react.

Arthur Hamilton had seen his share of crime shows. "You want me to wear a wire?"

"I thought of that, but no. Not if you are meeting in the Rose Plaza café."

"You're the boss."

"And please call me as soon as you have anything. Just to set your mind at ease, we have other potential suspects we're pursuing."

"Who's that?"

"Can't tell you." Of course, the other suspects were potentially Long Nugent's killer, not the Major's. Caryl hung up. He would dearly want to be the fly on the wall overhearing the conversation. Sometimes you just had to sit and wait and worry.

Chapter Thirty-nine

Caryl and J.J. still had nothing concrete. Caryl took the cover off the white board in his office and pondered. Then he got a surprise visit from the Assistant District Attorney, Mike McDaniel.

McDaniel had worked in the DA's office ever since the government cut funds for free lawyers. He went from defending the indigent to prosecuting generations of petty criminals. A graduate of the University of Oregon law school, he had been forced by circumstances to shift from idealism to semi-social worker. He didn't like the obligatory sentencing that erupted when states turned to commercialized prisons that depended on a steady stream of customer inmates. He had learned to work both sides of the law.

Though McDaniel was already fifty years old, he retained a smooth-faced boyish look Unlike Charlie Phung, troubles didn't imprint on McDaniel's face. Instead of sitting in Caryl's visitor's chair, he sat on the corner of the desk and looked at the white board. "What have you got on the Hamilton murder?"

Caryl wished J.J. was there, too, to back him up. "We're sure the murder of Major Hamilton is linked to Long Nguen, the strangled sex worker. It was her face on the selfie we found on the Major's cell phone. Whoever saw it published in the newspaper and on television decided to take action instead of letting us know her identity. I think she knew who might have killed the Major."

"But she was a sex worker. Any of her johns might have killed her."

"I don't think so. She had a regular clientele. The Major was her Friday trick. She also had a Thursday and a Wednesday client. We're checking them out. She wasn't trolling 82nd street."

"Not that you know of."

"True, but she was more of a high class call girl. Advertised in Willamette Week as a sex therapist. By appointment only."

McDaniel was studying the photos on the white board, especially the dragon tattoo on Long's pudenda. "And she was dumped up at Rocky Butte?"

"Right, but it wasn't your usual killing of a hooker. No robbery. Her ID was left at the scene. Whoever killed her wanted it to be known. I think the perp was making an example of her. "

"You think." The sarcasm was heavy.

"I think the perp wanted her death to be a warning to other would be sex workers."

McDaniel didn't agree. "Every sex worker knows how dangerous the profession is. They don't need any warnings. What about the Major? I see you noted this as a ritual murder. That a warning, too?"

Caryl didn't know.

McDaniel got up from the corner of Caryl's desk. "Fox, you ain't got shit. You want me to go to a grand jury with this? Guesses? Assumptions?"

It made Caryl feel foolish. This was his first big case. If he screwed this up the chief might send him back to vice, patrolling 82nd street and looking for drugged up, exhausted hookers terrified of their pimps and desperate for a twenty dollar blow job. "In the case of the Major, I think this is a revenge killing. Check out that black and white print from Vietnam. It was on a roll of film in the Major's safety deposit box. Similar killing."

"So? That was what, forty years ago?"

"Yes, but we have a witness."

Now McDaniel stared at Caryl's eyes with that same searching look some people gave him when they were deciding whether this was the face of a woman or a man. "Tell me about it."

"Major Hamilton got the Silver Star for rescuing an injured GI who lost his feet to a grenade. Name is Vaughn Swenson. He's one of the GIs in the photographs. He saw everything."

"You sure?"

"Look in the corner of the photo. There's a kid watching from the bushes. It looks to me like they were killing everyone in the village. The kid might have been shot, too."

"So?"

"So how about if that kid is still alive and living in Portland?"

"That your witness? You've got to be kidding me, Fox."

"No. Vaughn Swenson, the GI the Major rescued. He's the witness. He lives in Salem."

"Would he testify before a grand jury?"

Caryl hung his head. "Can't. When I showed him that photo he had a flash back. PTSD. He's back in a mental ward. Now the VA is on my case for being insensitive and tormenting a disabled veteran. They had to admit him."

McDaniel nodded. "The chief showed me the complaint. She also showed me the bill for the photos."

Caryl had his own flashback of sitting in a parked patrol car watching 82nd street. He tried to recover. "The apartment next to the Major's is being remodeled by Chang Construction. The foreman of the remodel crew is Charlie Phung, a Vietnamese."

"Did you question him?"

"J.J. and I had him in on an informal basis. He's nervous, says next time he'll bring his lawyer."

"Has he a rap sheet? Sounds like he expects trouble."

Caryl hadn't yet checked Phung's background. Now he felt foolish and careless. He gambled and said no. He didn't dare say his suspicions were based on Phung's body language. McDaniel would laugh him out of the office.

McDaniel shook his head. "All you have is suspicion and speculation, Fox. You have no evidence we can take to a Grand Jury."

His inexperience was showing. Caryl felt like a kid who just flunked the final exam and had been sent to the principal's office for cheating. He tried to wriggle out of it.. "There's another complication. Maybe I shouldn't mention this."

McDaniel was losing patience. "What?"

"Charlie Phung is the local expert on tracing Vietnamese ancestry. Major Hamilton's son is adopted and needs Phung to help him locate his birth mother."

"You're going to let this hunt for his mommy hinder your murder investigation?"

"Not necessarily. But if we assisted Arthur Hamilton, it would make a good human interest story if he finds her. Nice brownie points for the Portland Police helping out the Vietnamese community."

McDaniel clutched his head in frustration. "We're here to solve crimes, Fox. This ain't no genealogy web site. Arrest that Charlie Phung on suspicion of murder. Bring him in. Give him some heat and see if he cracks. A confession would be nice."

Chapter Forty

Caryl wanted Arthur Hamilton to have his chance at Charlie Phung first, so decided to wait until after that appointment in the Rose Plaza deli.

The deli was a small place on the second floor. Half a dozen tables provided a meeting place for residents and off duty staff. The back of the room was a grocery store, like a 7-11, just basics and no fresh meat or vegetables, but they did offer sandwiches from the Plaza kitchen and a daily soup.

There was no emergency exit from the deli.. The long hallways of the Plaza offered no refuge where he could hang out unobserved. He didn't want his presence to spook Charlie Phung. The best he could do was arrive early and stay out of sight in the display of canned goods.

He also needed a backup, a uniformed policeman to stand by when he made the arrest. A uniform was too conspicuous. He and the uniformed officer arrived together in an unmarked and conferred in the lobby. Before going up in the elevator to the second floor, Caryl told the uniform to go to the landing outside the north elevators and wait there. This was beyond the Plaza restaurant which blocked the view. There were a couple of soft chairs there where someone could wait out of sight of the lobby. When the time came, Caryl would call on his radio.

So he waited, hidden at the back of the deli. Looking over the top of a display he was able to watch as Arthur Hamilton took a table for two closest to the store display. He hoped he would be able to overhear their conversation. It was a noisy place.

How long could he pretend to be checking prices on cans of beans without being noticed?

Charlie Phung arrived a few minutes late and joined Arthur Hamilton. Arthur had his Vietnamese documents ready and showed them, took notes as Phung translated.

Then who should appear among the groceries but that snoopy Mrs. Seller with her green beret. She immediately recognized Caryl behind the canned goods display. "Why, Detective Fox! Are you shopping here at the Plaza deli?"

Caryl put his fingers to his lips.

The old amateur detective understood immediately. "You're on a stake out."

"Shh."

"I think you'll find better prices at Fred Meyer."

Caryl felt the best way to get rid of her was to enlist her services. "See those two at the table? The Vietnamese gentleman?"

She nodded knowingly.

"Don't approach them. Buy a cup of coffee and sit with your back to them while you listen to what they're saying. Just don't approach them."

Her eyes widened and she adjusted her beret to a conspiratorial angle. "You want me to be a witness?"

As they might say in court later, Caryl didn't affirm or deny.

With studied casualness that didn't quite conceal her stealth, Mrs. Seller paid for a cup of coffee and took a seat within earshot of the conversation going on between Phung and Hamilton.

Caryl watched carefully. When it looked like the meeting was almost over he radioed the uniformed cop to join him in the deli on the second floor right away.

Unfortunately, the policeman wasn't familiar with the layout of the Rose Plaza. He called for one of the north elevators and pushed the button for the second floor. What he didn't know was the assisted living annex over the parking garages had four floors over the three floors of garage. The ground floor was LP-1 for the parking garage street level. The floor marked two was the second floor of the assisted living. The floor marked three for the annex became the second floor for the twelve story tower end of the long building. The policeman was lost.

Charlie Phung was leaving the deli. Caryl could not wait any longer for his backup and approached him. "Charlie Phung?"

Phung immediately read Caryl's body language and might have fled, but there was no other exit from the deli.

"Charlie Phung, I'm arresting you on suspicion of the murder of Major Aaron Hamilton." Though Caryl had memorized the Miranda card text, he was so nervous that he stumbled and had to get it out of his wallet. He had almost finished reading Phung his rights when the breathless uniform showed up.

Charlie Phung reached for his cell phone. "I'm calling my lawyer."

While the uniform led him away Caryl spoke with Arthur Hamilton. "Did you get what you want?"

Hamilton wasn't sure. "I got the name and the dates. He says there's a data base."

Caryl shook his hand. "Good luck. You said your father was a war criminal. You might be called as a witness if this goes to trial."

"If?"

Caryl's face was pinched. He was afraid of making a mistake, afraid of failure. "It's suspicion. You never know."

He glanced over Arthur's shoulder at Mrs. Seller. She looked like the cat that swallowed the canary. She was fairly bursting with excitement at having been a witness to the arrest. How long before everyone in the Rose Plaza knew her story?

Chapter Forty-one

The routine of booking Charlie Phung was intended to
intimidate him. His photograph was taken, front and
profile. His fingerprints were taken. He had to hand over
the contents of his pockets, his wallet, his cell phone, his
watch-- everything put into a heavy envelope and signed
for. The psychological effect was intended to render him
powerless in the face of police authority. He wasn't
intimidated.

Then they made him wait. Actually, they had to hold
off the interrogation until J.J. arrived from the east
precinct. They also had to wait for Phung's lawyer.

Phung's lawyer, Than Li, according to his business
card, was a specialist in immigration law. The business
card had a caption in three languages, English, what
appeared to be Vietnamese, and Spanish. He was a
Vietnamese-American, second generation, who had
moved to Oregon from California where most of his
clients were Mexican, so his third language was Spanish.
He was younger than Phung. He also thought the reason
he was called in was because of some difficulty with
Phung's status. Criminal law was not his specialty.

This time the interview would take place in a formal
setting with a one way glass window so McDaniel could
wait and watch. Everything would be recorded and
filmed.

Caryl began with basic background questions. First
he confirmed Charlie Phung's identity, his nationality, his
address, his employer, everything that went into a basic
dossier.

Phung had immigrated to the United States after the
war. He met his wife at a relocation camp. He was
married, had twins, a boy and a girl, both students at

PCC, Portland Community College. He had no criminal record.

He was also the president of the Vietnamese Orphans' Association, a charitable group that assisted victims of the war and helped people with adoptions.

Charlie Phung was an exemplary naturalized US citizen.

That established, Caryl got into the murder of Major Hamilton. At this point, Phung was evasive. No, he did not know Aaron Hamilton. He had seen him only once by chance in the hallway. Caryl asked, "Did you know that Hamilton had served in Vietnam?"

"How would I know that? I didn't know the man. He was just someone who lived on the twelfth floor of the Rose Plaza."

"'Did you know that Major Hamilton was a war criminal?"

Charlie Phung knew about one case. "You mean like the My Lai incident? Lieutenant Calli who killed all those women and babies?"

"Right." Caryl had done his homework and looked p Vietnam War atrocities.

"Was Mr. Hamilton at My Lai?"

"No." Caryl looked at J.J. She frowned. He realized Phung had a way of turning questions back with questions of his own. He decided on another line of questioning. "You do know Arthur Hamilton. He is the Major's son?"

"I am helping him find his birth mother. She is Vietnamese."

"Arthur Hamilton said his father was a war criminal. They were not on speaking terms."

"I did not know that."

Caryl was sure Phung knew more than he was admitting. So far he had been evasive. Caryl reached for his ever present folder of crime scene photographs. "Arthur Hamilton had an album of souvenir photographs of his time in the war, the usual buddy soldier pictures. But we also found a roll of film in his father's safety deposit box. We had prints made. These were not in his album. They were too incriminating."

Charlie Phung's face showed no emotion. "So?"

Caryl took out the worst one, the one of the then lieutenant Hamilton and his prisoner. It was the same vivid trigger photograph that put Swensen back in the psycho ward at the VA. How would Phung react?

Caryl and J.J. watched Phung intensely to see his reaction.

This time Charlie Phung was shocked. His voice trembled. "How did you get this?"

"One of Hamilton's men had a camera, apparently fancied himself as a war correspondent. These photos could never be shown to the public."

Phung wasn't able to speak. He took out his handkerchief, wiped his forehead, blew his nose. Finally gathering himself, he managed to say, "That is Hamilton."

"So you know Hamilton."

"I did not know him then. I only knew he was an American officer."

"So you were there?"

Charlie Phung swallowed and nodded. "The man Hamilton is torturing in the photo is my grandfather."

"And you saw this? You were there?"

"I am the boy in the bushes." He pointed to the nearly hidden figure at the side of the frame.

"What happened then?"

Charlie Phung was reliving the experience. Remembering, he took a deep breath. "I had a grenade. When I saw my grandfather was dead, I threw it and ran for the Viet Kong."

Charlie looked at J.J. "That must be how Swenson lost his feet." To Phung, "What happened then?"

"Viet Kong came. Most of the Americans were killed. I learned that a helicopter came and took some away."

"Hamilton got a medal for bravery."

"Hamilton was a murderer. You know how many old people and children were murdered in our village? Thirty-five. I was the only one who escaped. It was never reported."

Caryl had been in the military but only briefly until he was discharged. He had not experienced war. When he said, "It was war," the words were meaningless, a hollow platitude, like referring to collateral damage, as if war could be an excuse for atrocities.

Charlie Phung was barely able to speak. "We were not Viet Kong. We were only farmers. It was murder."

Caryl could say nothing. What did he know about the horrors that put Swensen in the hospital with PTSD? His own worst experience in the military was being ridiculed and beaten up because he wanted a sex change.

"There was no justice," Phung said. "There has to be justice."

Caryl looked up at the window which he knew McDaniel was behind, watching. "Do you think the murder of Major Hamilton was justice?"

Charlie Phung might have spoken, but his lawyer cautioned him. "My client has no comment."

"So what did you do? Track Hamilton down through military records so you could exact your revenge?"

"No comment."

"Do you think you have the right, the authority, to be judge, jury and executioner for a war criminal?"

"No comment."

"Did you murder Aaron Hamilton?"

"No comment."

J.J. had her turn. "Long Nguen was a sex worker who serviced Major Hamilton. She was strangled and her body dumped at Rocky Butte. What do you know about that?"

"No comment."

"Did you kill Long Nguen?"

"The girl was a disgrace to our community."

"Did you kill her?"

"She deserved what she got."

J.J. persisted. "But did you kill her?"

Charlie Phung shook his head.

Caryl ended the interrogation. He would have to confer with McDaniel. Phung had the motive and the opportunity to kill Major Hamilton, but unless he confessed, how well would this go down with a jury?

Caryl pondered the situation. What would he have done if he were the only witness to his grandfather's murder? What if there was no justice, but only revenge? When an active shooter killed all those people at the black church, they actually forgave him. Could he? Or was forgiveness the purview of God? Hokanson's church had the sign "Hate the sin, love the sinner." Arthur Hamilton hated his father. He did not even plan to attend the graveside service. Why not?

Attending the graveside service would provide closure. A funeral wasn't for the deceased. It was for those who still lived so they could go on with their lives. Charlie Phung had never gotten over his grandfather's murder. Should he? They say that your experience at age ten defines your lifetime view of the world. That was about how old Charlie Phung had been when he witnessed the rampage of American soldiers in a frenzy of blood lust.

People say you have to move on. Those were empty words for people like Swenson and Charlie Phung. They were trapped in their own nightmares.

Caryl was satisfied that he had got as close as he could for now, for a confession. But what about Long Nguen? She was murdered, too. Was that some kind of justice, too? If so, what?

Chapter forty-two

Charlie Phung was taken back to his cell. There would be an arraignment and a request for bail.

J.J. and Caryl joined McDaniel in the observation room. For once, McDaniel was pleased with Caryl's work. "You got him. Well done."

Caryl felt a huge sense of relief. Yes, Phung had the motive and the opportunity, and he probably did the ritual murder, but there was more to it than that. "He's going to plead not guilty."

"No surprise."

Caryl could nor forget Swenson's reaction to the photograph. "Phung's going to turn the murder into a war crimes case. It's going to be a Vietnam war victim against the United States. In the discovery phase he's going to present all those photographs. I would not be surprised if, like those abused women who kill their husbands, that it is justified homicide."

McDaniel was skeptical. For him it was open and shut. He didn't even need a confession. The jury would convict Phung of first degree murder.

"He's not the only one on trial," Caryl suggested. "He's the president of the Vietnam Orphan's Association. A trial will bring in the entire Vietnamese community."

McDaniel obviously didn't like that. "We'll have to limit the case to the crime itself. Leave out the Vietnam war incident."

J.J. had a different view. "Not if they play the race card. The Vietnamese may have won the war, but their people were the victims. Don't be surprised if there's a demonstration, 'Free Charlie Phung!' I can just see it."

Caryl agreed. "He only did what the US government failed to do in the case of a war criminal. He also has a witness who saw the whole thing.

McDaniel disagreed. "I saw the complaint from the VA. For compassionate reasons, Swenson cannot be forced to appear."

"You think this could turn into a side show? National TV? The Vietnam war on trial again? With a local population of ten thousand Vietnamese immigrants? Don't be so sure."

McDaniel sat back in his chair and fiddled with a pencil. He'd been doodling, a little series of pictures of hangman's nooses.

"It'll be harder to charge Phung with the murder of the sex worker unless we get a confession. Maybe that DNA evidence will pin him down."

McDaniel shook his head. "I saw the crime lab report. Inconclusive. All she had under her fingernails was dirt from Rocky Butte."

Caryl sat at the observers' table with his head in his hands. He had finally got to Major Hamilton's killer. Murder one should be good for thirty years. He had proved himself as a homicide detective. But would it stick? Not every arrest led to a conviction and not every conviction ended in jail time. Nothing was simple.

J.J. saw his uncertainty but didn't have enough experience to offer a solution or even the right words.

McDaniel did. "We had a similar case here in Portland. A grandmother in a family of low lifes had been abused for years. We knew that from numerous calls about domestic violence. Finally she killed her husband. We knew she could get thirty years but we had a long discussion with the judge."

J.J. was incredulous. "You mean she got off?"

McDaniel shook his head. "We couldn't do that. It was murder."

Caryl look up. "What? Justifiable homicide?"

"We can't give every abused wife license to kill. We plea bargained for a ten year sentence. The old lady was out on parole in three."

J.J. and Caryl looked at each other, considering that alternative in the case of Charlie Phung.

McDaniel wasn't finished. "I understood their situation. We established a relationship with that family. They turned their lives around. The granddaughter is actually earning money for college working part time in my office. She wants to be a P.O."

J.J. asked, "P.O?"

"Parole officer."

Caryl saw the point of that. Reformed drug addicts sometimes became drug counselors. O.G.s, Old Gangsters, those who survived, sometimes worked in rehabilitation of gangs. There was more than one path to justice.

McDaniel shoved his notes into his own case file folder. "I'll confer with Phung's lawyer. Offer a plea bargain. If he accepts, we'll save the county the cost of a jury trial."

J.J.'s job wasn't done. "What about the murder of Long Nguen?"

"Better show up at the next meeting of the Vietnamese Orphans' Association. Those murders were connected. I bet someone there knows something. "

Caryl offered, "I'll go with you. I'll bet that old lady gatekeeper will finger someone."

Chapter Forty-three

The body of Major Hamilton was handed over to the crematorium. Arthur Hamilton didn't wait for the cremains. Aaron Hamilton had prepaid the cremation and left instructions for internment in the National Cemetery east of Portland. Arthur had finished clearing out his father's apartment and handed over the keys to Mrs. Grafton. As for the Major's car, Arthur had no need for it and wasn't about to drive across country back to Syracuse, New York. Instead, on advice from Ms. Grafton, he called Oregon Public Broadcasting and gave them the car. The transactions were completed quickly.

There were people on the Rose Plaza waiting list that wanted that choice apartment with a view of the park. Chang Construction would do the remodeling to the new tenant's specifications.

There would be no sign that Aaron Hamilton had ever been there. Few of the Plaza residents knew him. He did not register on anyone's long term memory. As for Mrs. Seller, the Plaza's resident amateur detective, Major Hamilton's murder would soon be old gossip nobody cared about..

But what about the murder of Long Nguen? J,J called Caryl at the precinct to keep him informed of her progress. Lotus Nguen said her father was making arrangements for Long's funeral, but her mother was not willing to face others in the Vietnamese community who knew her daughter was a sex worker.

J.J. had made no progress on the murder itself. Sex workers were easy prey for serial killers, like the Green River killer. There were over thirty thousand unsolved missing persons cases in the United States.

If Charlie Phung had killed her because she dishonored the community, he wasn't talking. Still, J.J. was going to have a last shot at the case and invited Caryl to join her at the next Association meeting.

The community center had not changed since their last visit, but now everyone knew J.J. and Caryl. Though the judge's decision had not been made public, they also knew about the plea bargain and seemed satisfied.

J.J. was invited to the podium to make her pitch. "The Portland Police are still looking for clues to who may have killed Long Nguen. If you know anything at all about it, please call me at the Second Precinct." She wrote her number in chalk on the worn blackboard and handed out her business card.

Would anybody call in a tip? Crime Stoppers offered a $2500 reward for information that led to an arrest and conviction.

They didn't have long to wait. The next day it began, not mere tips, but confessions. It was well known that some people would confess to a crime they didn't commit. They were what? Crackpots? People wanting a moment of fame? Apparently not in this case. Thirty-two Vietnamese members of the Orphan's Association confessed to the murder of Long Nguen.

Apparently they had conferred, for their stories matched. They had all lured Lung Nguen to Rocky Butte and killed her. They said they had beaten her to death with baseball bats and clubs. Of course, she had been strangled with her own panties, a detail the police had not revealed. The confessions were all bogus.

Caryl thought the mass confession might have been because they had guilty consciences for having disrespected Long. After all, it was because of her that the Association had been given that big bequest by Major Hamilton. They might also have confessed to protect Charlie Phung.

It looked like the murder of Long Nguen would be another cold case to add to Detective Casey's old filing cabinet in Caryl's office.

As the excitement died down, Caryl called J.J. and invited her to lunch at Fong's Chinese restaurant. She could have a seafood plate. Very halal. He had news for her.

They walked from the First Precinct to Fong's and were seated at Caryl's regular table. The restaurant was almost deserted. Mr. Fong waited on them himself. He was grateful to see the detective again and reported, sadly, that traffic in the Old Town was in decline. He would soon close the restaurant. It was time he thought about retiring.

J.J. looked very smart in her head scarf. It made Caryl wonder what her hair was like. Did she take the requirement of Muslim modesty too seriously? He asked, "Do you always cover your hair?"

She smiled. "Not always. I started wearing a head covering when our chief investigator wanted me to dress like a hooker decoy on 82nd street in a sting to catch johns. I didn't want to be a decoy, said going without the scarf was against my religion. Johns aren't interested in Muslim women." She winked.

For J.J. modest dress was a rule. Caryl saw that they both had ways of protecting their identity. "I guess we all wear costumes of a sort." He did, too, avoiding anything that looked feminine.

Sipping her little cup of green tea, J.J. asked, "So what's your news? You said you had something for me."

"It was just an excuse to see you again," Caryl said. Then he sheepishly added, backing off from the flirtation, "I heard from Arthur Hamilton. You know I went to his father's graveside service. I was the only spectator. The honor guard had no one to give the American flag to, so I took it and sent it to him. He actually thanked me for it." It looked to Caryl that Arthur Hamilton had finally found closure.

"Nice of you. You're a good guy Caryl."

"Thanks for the guy part. That's not the news, though. Arthur Hamilton has found his birth mother. He's flying to Vietnam to meet her. Would you believe:

she works in a textile factory making shirts to sell at Wal-Mart."

They were silent for a along moment. Caryl thought of Swenson. The disabled veteran was back in Salem, still struggling with his PTSD. "Just think, J.J., we killed two and a half million Vietnamese, lost the war, and now we're buying shirts from them. Go figure.

Chapter Forty-Four

When the case was over and Charlie Phung transported to Umatillo prison Hal McDaniel, coffee cup and Danish in hand, let himself into Caryl Fox's office, closed the door, and sat down in the visitor's chair. "You lucked out on the Phung case, Detective."

"How's that?"

"You botched the crime scene investigation."

"Oh?"

"There had to be a lot of blood. I saw the pictures."

Caryl was defensive. "What do you mean?"

"Phung's footprints showed he had to be wearing booties. I wouldn't be surprised if he was wearing a bunny suit."

"Bunny suit?"

"Disposable paper coveralls like those used by painters and guys working in fiberglass plants. He'd have been blood all over and have to ditch the coveralls someplace. You didn't look?"

Caryl swallowed. "But we got a conviction."

"There had to be clues in a Chang Construction van."

"Chang Construction has a fleet of vans."

"So next time, check them all out."

Caryl felt stupid. Did this mean he was going back to Vice? "Sorry."

McDaniel finished his coffee. "No sweat, Caryl. You did good, you got the guy. Next time you'll do better."

Caryl felt relieved.

McDaniel gave him a rare smile as he got up to leave. "We all make mistakes sometimes. Welcome to the club, Caryl."

The End

Feedback

Your thoughts about this book would be appreciated. Why not send an email to the author, Harley l. Sachs, at <u>sachsharley@gmail.com</u>. Suggested questions to start with are:

1) What did you like best about this book?
2) What did you like least?
3) Would you like to see more stories about Caryl and J.J.?
4) If you liked this book, would you post a review at Amazon.com?

About Harley L. Sachs:

Harley L. Sachs is the author of many novels, short stories, magazine articles and newspaper columns. His short stories have been broadcast on the BBC World Service short wave and on Oregon Public Radio's Golden Hours.
He now lives with his wife Ulla in Portland, Oregon.

Dead Men Don't Bleed is the seventh in the Mystery Club Rose Plaza series. For more stories about Katherine Seller and her team of amateur sleuths, you could start with *The Mystery Club Solves a Murder*. Here's a sample:

1. What the Crows Found

For the first morning in a week it was not raining in Portland. At last Mary Higgins might catch sight of the rumored Peregrine falcons.

Wearing her green, hooded rain jacket and using her gold headed cane for support she had climbed painfully up the South Broadway grade to a vantage point for a clear view. There was another spot higher up, but the climb was formidable. The shoulder of the winding road was so narrow there was no room for a person on foot to stand out of the way of the traffic.

Mary had forgotten how heavy her binoculars could be. Her grand nephew Charlie had given her a light weight pair of 10 power birder's binoculars for her eightieth birthday, but she found them difficult to hold steady. Instead she stuck to the 7 by 50's, a sentimental souvenir from her days as an RAF pilot in World War II. That was nearly sixty years ago. Her legs were a lot stronger then, and her hands steady, not trembling with the onset of Parkinson's. You had to be tough to be old.

She rested against the guard rail at the edge of the steep street to catch her breath. The Plaza was down below, a long, twelve story zigzag building that housed her and nearly three hundred other retirees, mostly women. From here she could see the Plaza roof, look down into the parking lot between it and the hill where she now stood, and beyond to the Willamette River and south east Portland. On clear days Mount Hood was visible, its classic volcano shape crowned with snow all year.

A bird soared above one of the Oregon Health Sciences University buildings high on the hill above her. Was it the falcon someone had said they saw? There was a nesting pair in a skyscraper near Lloyd's Center on the other side of the river, doing a nice business in pigeons. But what about this side of the Willamette?

Even without using the binoculars Mary Higgins could see it was a hawk. She wasn't sure which. Occasionally a flock of sea gulls would circle the park after heavy rains, foraging for earthworms driven up out of their hiding places in the turf. Today there were no gulls, but a pair of crows interested in something. What was it?

One of the crows settled cautiously on the Plaza parapet. She focused the 7 by 50's on the parapet. The roof was covered with heavy, red gravel, except where it was set up as a patio. On days when it wasn't raining, residents could sun themselves and enjoy the view.

The other crow was interested in something down on the roof between the old wing of the Plaza and the new extension. Mary could see the notch between the two sections of the Plaza from this vantage point. What were the crows after?

Mary Higgins leaned over the guard rail to get a better angle with the binoculars. Now the other crow had left the parapet and joined its partner to peck at something. She knew crows were garbage birds, carrion eaters, but there was little road kill here in the city. Crows were reduced to foraging the Park Blocks trash cans or the dumpsters. What had they found on the Plaza roof?

It looked like a bundle of laundry, something white. If she could just hold the binoculars steady.... Crows wouldn't be interested in a bundle of rags. Mary shifted her weight and steadied her elbows against her stomach. It looked like...

The blast of a car horn and the crunch of gravel startled her. An ATV with big wheels and a thumping stereo narrowly missed her. She felt herself teetering, about to fall over the railing. Her cane slipped off the guard rail and clattered onto the gravel. She pulled herself back to safety doubly chilled. It was not only the fear of being struck by a car or falling down the bluff that sent a chill across her fragile shoulders. It was what the crows had found-- it looked like a body on the roof.

Mary Higgins picked up her cane and hurried down the Broadway grade as fast as her painful knees would tolerate. She had seen corpses before, at the airfield in England-- shattered airmen dragged from burning aircraft-- and remembered the stench of scorched bodies. The associations jumbled together in her mind, the fear, the horror, and the loss.

She needed a closer look at the crows' find to make sure. The view from the roof should do it.

Here's a list of books by Harley L. Sachs:

MYSTERY NOVELS

The Mystery Club Series

THE MYSTERY CLUB SOLVES A MURDER

First and most popular of the Mystery Club series. Mary Higgins finds the body of Dora Reed on the roof of the Plaza retirement building, notifies the police, then tells the Mystery Club. They assume several suspects: the manager of the Plaza, Dora's son Donald, or a Plaza employee. Dora's husband, Ed Sutherland, is in Hawaii on board the yacht Miss Chief with an all girl crew. Carrying on their own investigation, the Mystery Club finally suspects Sutherland, though he seems to have a perfect alibi. If they can prove it to their satisfaction, will a court ever convict him-- if he can be found somewhere in the Pacific?

THE MYSTERY CLUB AND THE DEAD DOCTOR

Second in the Mystery Club series. The Mystery Club consists of five elderly women who live at the Rose Plaza and discuss mysteries written by women. The Mystery Club ladies have no idea of the consequences when Viola Cartwright, their blind member, asks them to go over her Medicare bills. That leads to suspicion about the identity of her personal assistant, Dorothy Anderson, who turns out to be using a stolen identity. Viola's doctor runs a phony clinic owned by a member of the Russian Mafia. Soon the investigation of Medicare bills leads to murder and tragedy, stopped only by the courage of Mary Higgins.

THE MYSTERY CLUB AND THE HIDDEN WITNESS

Third in the Mystery Club series. The ladies of the Mystery Club discover one of the residents is a crook under WITSEC, the witness protection program. He apparently keeps dipping into the employee gift fund. The Mystery Club bands together to track down the missing money, but what they discover is danger.

THE MYSTERY CLUB AND THE SERIAL WIDOW

Fourth in the Mystery Club series. Caroline Kostinsky, new resident at the Rose Plaza, is a widow four times over and she's looking for a fifth husband in retired General Hardcastle, but when drunk she says she killed all of her husbands. Except for her confession, there's no evidence. Now what?

DELIVER ME FROM EVIL

Responding to a posted invitation for new members for the Mystery Club, Judge Ira Kahane and Ursula Besette show up. Ursula, at a turning point in her life as a new Rose Plaza resident, is interested in Wicca and Kabala. Roberta Nelson believes one should not suffer a witch to live. Judge Kahane tries to lead Ursula on the right path, but there is conflict and tragedy coming.

WHITE SLAVE

Sequel to *The Mystery Club Solves a Murder*. The appearance of Ed Sutherland's gold bracelet in a Portland pawn shop revives retired detective Casey's interest in the cold case. He doesn't know that Sutherland has been picked up and is a slave on a Korean fishing boat. Sutherland, penniless, .without clothes or identification, is stranded in New Zealand. Can he find his way back to Portland and be somehow redeemed or face a death sentence for first degree murder?

DEAD MEN DON'T BLEED

Another murder at the Rose Plaza: It isn't easy being the only transgender male detective in the Portland, Oregon police force in spite of the city's reputation as friendly to gay, lesbian and transsexual people. That's the experience of Caryl (previously Carol) Fox who transferred out of Vice because he could no longer stand the pedophiles, pimps, drug dealers, meth addicts, hookers and sex traffickers. His experience was not so different from his sometimes partner in arms, J.J. an unabashedly young woman who converted to Islam and wore her head covering even if it was accompanied by a bulletproof vest. She continued to labor in Vice while Caryl Fox was yet to prove his Homicide abilities in a puzzling murder case. In the Hamilton/Nguen double murder case, their integrity and skills as detectives was about to be tested.

The Irwin Glass Series

BETRAYAL

Prequel to *Retribution*. Irwin Glass, BA in Russian, MA in International Relations, has a promising career in the Foreign Service in Moscow until he is snared in a classic "honey pot" seduction. He's young and naïve, honest, always wants to do the right thing, but at every turn he is betrayed. The incident in Moscow destroys his career. He is accused of being a paid Soviet agent and is pursued by the consequences of his encounter with the KGB twenty years later. Some enemies never let go

RETRIBUTION

Sequel to *Betrayal*. Newly married to Ivy Hartshorn, Irwin Glass gets a dunning letter from the IRS for taxes on interest at the Washington, DC account he didn't think he had. It's a joint account with his missing birth daughter and the balance is huge. Assuming it's money Katya's KGB father of record, Vladimir Putinsky (now Putin) deposited for her living expenses, Irwin moves it to force her to contact him. But Ivy warns him that he is laundering money and the people it belongs to will come after him. Irwin's complicated life is catching up with him, but this time he will find retribution.

BURNT OUT

Irwin Glass is approached by FBI Agent Wilkins who asks for Irwin's lists of foreign students. Not satisfied he wants more and is looking for potential terrorists among the Moslem students. Gradually Irwin is sucked into the role of FBI informant on the Michigan Institute of Technology's Muslim Students' Association and the results are tragic.

THE IRWIN GLASS TRILOGY

All three Irwin Glass books in one package deal. The Irwin Glass Trilogy combines all three of the Irwin Glass Mysteries: "Betrayal," "Retribution," and "Burnt Out," following the chaotic career of Irwin Glass who began, in "Betrayal," as a state department clerk in Moscow only to be caught in a classic honey pot seduction. Betrayed at every turn, he was sent back to the United States in disgrace to try to start a new life. No such luck. His teaching career is upturned by the revelation that the Moscow seduction had a consequence in the form of a beautiful student Katya who claims to be his daughter. In "Retribution," Irwin's KGB nemesis is in the United States seeking political asylum, but in fact is fleeing the Russian Mafia with Irwin as quarry. After "Retribution," Irwin thinks he is home free of all that intrigue, but the local FBI agent has a hold on him and wants information about potential terrorists among Irwin's students at Michigan Institute of Technology. There are risks to being a reluctant FBI informant, and Irwin's reports may be misconstrued with tragic results. What Irwin and his wife really want is a normal life, but his mysterious Russian birth daughter Katya remains an enigma. Is she or isn't she?

Other Mysteries

MURDER BY MAIL

German exchange student Klaus Hitz is more interested in making money than in asking questions about his work assignment. He doesn't know that the industrialist father of his punk girl friend is using him in a terrorist conspiracy to kill everyone in the United States with a mass mailing of a scratch and sniff virus. The plot begins to unravel when a Polish nurse brings blood samples from Libya and alerts a CIA agent. While the CIA and FBI track down the terrorists, Klaus Hitz gradually figures it out. How can he avoid being murdered or imprisoned for being naive?

MURDER IN THE KEWEENAW

CIA agent recovering from Post traumatic Stress after failed missions in Finland and a divorce is fishing in Lake Superior when he snags a corpse. He thinks he has seen the girl before and his attempt to identify her leads him to a ring of deadly pornographers. It almost costs him his own life.

CONSPIRACY!

Technical writer Tom Godot can't believe his luck when CONSPIRACY!, the book he has co-written with the elusive Harold Stevenson, is a hit. The book details a plot to hijack communication satellites. As Tom crosses the country on his book tour, he is disturbed by people interested in early drafts and dogged by an NSA agent.

Communicating by fax with his editor and by encrypted e-mail with the mysterious Stevenson, Tom reaches out in his loneliness to his California girl friend Sylvia Hanson who turns out to be a pivotal figure. There is another conspiracy, and Tom is part of it

THE GOLD CHROMOSOME

When Adam Rottman's childless Aunt Sadie Gold died, the eight cousins learned her estate was in an irrevocable trust, the proceeds going to Adam's sister Sarah while she lives. After Sarah's death, the money would go to the last surviving cousin. It's a fatal tontine Adam's lawyer brother Harold set up. Would the cousins kill each other for one million dollars? Sarah's car is found in the river, but not Sarah. That begins a series of mysterious deaths. Coincidence? Or Murder? Who will be next? Adam and his psychologist wife Deborah must stop the chain before he, too, is eliminated.

BEN ZAKKAI'S COFFIN

Born of a Jewish father and a Catholic mother, Herman Bachrach insists he has no religion, but he is drawn by circumstance into a holocaust vendetta over gold stolen by a Swiss bank from Jewish depositors. Seduced by a woman who calls herself Diana, no last name, Herman is suspected by detective Sheehan to be her murderer. Someone else wants him dead. His Jewish boss provides him with a lawyer, but sends him to Switzerland to finish the job "Diana" started. It's an assignment he can't refuse. The result is an epiphany of identity that changes Herman's life forever.

THE LOLLIPOP MURDER

A warning for wannabe novelists! What happens when a stable of neurotic novelists who live in their pseudonyms and are bound by iron clad contracts are invited aboard their miserly Florida publisher's yacht for the Miami Book Fair only to find that they have no hope of ever earning a dime of royalties for their books? All this as Hurricane Gerta threatens to sink the yacht at the dock. It's grounds for murder

NOVELS

SAM IN LOVE

A coming of age romance for mature young adults. U.S. Army life in Europe in the 1950's was an equivalent of the Grand Tour of the eighteenth century when young men traveled and sowed wild oats. Marty, roommate of Sam Logan, a PFC draftee serving in the US Army in Munich, Germany, says all Sam needs is to get laid. Sam is not a virgin, but has a Midwestern ethic and believes in love. He doesn't know quite what that is. No Casanova, Sam, through a series of tentative encounters, thinks he's found the love of his life.

STOPRAPE.COM

Kerstin Mikkola, a young TV reporter at KDUP in Marquette, Michigan has hopes of a better network job. Her interview with a marine victim or rape might be just the ticket. Her interview about the web site StopRape.com goes viral on U-tube and Kerstin finds herself in the thick of consequences she did not anticipate.

THE ACCIDENTAL COURIER

A romance, road trip, and mystery all in one. Charles Kosko, retired orchard owner from Oregon, decides to take a bus trip in Europe and finds himself involved in a whistle-blower's scheme to discredit an American cell phone company that uses rare earths mined by slaves in the Congo. Unable to speak any foreign language, and without his US passport, he is picked up by a beautiful Israeli woman who says she is his driver. But is he really her prisoner? They are pursued by an African mining engineer, who hopes to intercept the delivery of stolen rare earths,

SCI-FI AND FANTASY

NEVER TRUST A TALKING HORSE

The narrator of this dystopian novel escapes preventive detention into a world he discovers has gone mad. Hungry, he is told he can eat for free at Lachumba's supper club, only to discover that he might be the main dish. He rescues Iris I. Iris from the ovens and in a series of episodes explores the insane world in search of a livelihood. He gradually realizes why he was incarcerated in the first place, but by then it is too late. His and Iris's roles have been reversed. Arrested, they are given a sadistic sentence which is their final challenge.

THE SEARCH FOR JESSE BRAM

Jesse Bram, the young hero of this metaphysical science fiction adventure, is unaware of his Jewish roots. An Eldre of mixed breed, he is marooned on the post apocalyptic shunned planet URth where technology and books have been destroyed. The URthlings variously view Jesse as a bringer of cargo for the half-breed prefect Hrod, as the reborn Savior by crypto-Christians, and as a link to the past by a remnant of Jews. The Galactic Federation suspects him of treason and he is pursued by an enigmatic Trinian policeman. If Jesse survives, will he be convicted? If acquitted, what next?

SHORT STORIES

THREADS OF THE COVENANT: THE JEWS OF RED JACKET

A collection of twenty-one short stories about Jewish life in small town America centering about two main characters, David Katz, the only Jewish boy in Red Jacket, and Richard Goldman, the only Jewish professor at Copper country Community College. Each story depicts another aspect of what it means to be a Jew in a small town as each character comes to realize his own identity.

MISPLACED PERSONS

Though set in different locales what these stories have in common is a central character who is out of his element, in the wrong place, coming to grips with cultural, generational, or physical displacement. In PROBLEM FOR THE TEACHER an expatriate fumbles for a living; in LIMBO an ex-G.I. is adrift in Copenhagen; in TRIUMPH OF THE WILL a nervous wreck seeks recuperation; in MISCALCULATION a would be tax evader succumbs to his own fears; in THE LIE a drunk gets himself into difficulties, and in THE GIRLS OF FREDERIKSHAVN an old man is trapped by girls looking for action.

YOOPER TALES AND OTHER FUNNY STUFF

Extracted from the massive volume of Sachs's published Essays and Columns: 1992-2011, this collection of stories related to Michigan's Upper Peninsula, known as the UP, home of Yoopers, reveals the truth about snow fleas, ice worms, the humungous fungus (world's largest living thing) and the rigors of winters in the remote north woods. You can also learn how to catch and cook the Mosquito Giganticus and why visitors won't come. Sachs has several awards for his humor.

AHOY! QUARTERDECK!

Originally published as IRMA QUARTERDECK REPORTS but re-released with new illustrations and, in the paperback edition, with sea shanties, this funny book is a series of boating anecdotes about Irma and her bumbling husband Ralph ("I can't believe I lost the anchor") Quarterdeck in their many boating adventures and mishaps. One reviewer says the book is as informative as Chapman's famous manual, but more fun. Readers will find plenty of laughs in this book and at the same time learn a great deal of boating fundamentals.

ANNA-LENA'S TROLL AND OHER STORIES

Each of the three Sachs daughters has a story in this children's book. "Anna-Lena's Troll" explores the nature of trolls, which represent the dark side of human behavior as Anna-Lena's nasty letter to Santa is rewarded by the gift of a nasty troll. "The Return of Baby Suzy" is the true story of Cynthia's worn out doll and its resurrection. "The Stars for Christmas" is the remarkable surprise Belinda got along with her new eye glasses. Other family stories are Christmas related.

NON-FICTION

THE MISADVENTURES OF CPL. SACHS

Adrift through college at Indiana University, author Sachs was drafted at the end of the Korean War. Physically unfit for combat, he was sent to Queer Company for basic training, then by a fluke was shipped out to Germany instead of Korea. Thus began his own version of the traditional Grand Tour.

FREELANCE NONFICTION ARTICLES

This third edition of a monograph on freelance writing first published by the Society for Technical Communication is newly updated. This little manual provides tips for interviewing, article structure, article preparation and submission, photography, and business practice.

CHILLY-CHILLY-BANG—HOW WE FREELANCED THROUGH EUROPE'S COLDEST WINTER IN A VW WITH A KID

Companion piece to *Freelance Nonfiction Articles*. The former is a how to book. This is a "how we did it" memoir. The author knew nothing about Volkswagens when they set off, but as they worked from VW dealer to dealer getting the old Combi fixed, he learned! It's as much a book for VW enthusiasts as it is for writers.

Both FREELANCE NONFICTION ARTICLES and *Chilly-Chilly-BANG! How we Freelanced Through Europe's Coldest Winter in a VW with a Kid* are combined in a double volume, *The Writing Life*.

THE 1957 SACHS ARCTIC EXPEDITION

After military service in Germany the author took the GI Bill to Sweden. With no income in the summer, and not even sure there was a road to the far north, he set off hitchhiking to North Cape, the northernmost point in Europe in search of the midnight sun. Illustrated.

FROM TENT TO CASTLE: MEMOIR OF A YEAR LONG HONEYMOON

Setting off from Stockholm, Sweden on rebuilt one speed bicycles, Harley and Ulla embarked on an open-ended honeymoon with no fixed destination and equipped with a tent, a thin double sleeping bag, a tiny gasoline stove, and $3000. After arriving in Britain, Ulla discovered she was pregnant. Tired of unrelenting rain, they advertised for a cheap place to spend the winter. They were offered the gatehouse to Borthwick Castle outside Edinburgh, Scotland for $25 a month by British author Theo Lang.

"IS"

As Bill Clinton said, "It all depends on what the meaning of "is" is."

A problem we all have is distinguishing between what is real and what is not. This is in fact an age-old question. This volume switches between classical instances of the problem to the author and his psychiatrist and his wife. What is real? That all depends on the meaning of "real."

QUEER COMPANY

Not a gay novel, this is a fictionalized memoir of an experimental basic training unit at the end of the Korean War. All the draftees were physically unfit for combat but the army didn't want to discharge them. Instead they got modified training in a company unfortunately designated Q. In the Army phonetic alphabet Q is Queen, but Q company was called queer. A copy is in the US Army historical archives.

www.ingramcontent.com/pod-product-compliance
Lightning Source LLC
Chambersburg PA
CBHW072124270326
41931CB00010B/1659